HENRIETTA TAYLOR grew up in Mosman, Sydney, and trained as a language teacher while travelling extensively around France and Italy. Her first book, *Escaping*, was published in 2007. She now owns and runs three rental cottages in Provence, in the south of France. Her spare time is spent failing miserably to train two black cats and two bilingual dogs. Her two bilingual children, Mimi and Harry, continue to give her handy hints about her shortcomings in motherhood.

GW00361801

Lavender & Linen

HENRIETTA TAYLOR

HARPER PERENNIAL

Harper Perennial
An imprint of HarperCollins*Publishers*

First published in Australia in 2007
This edition published in 2008
by HarperCollins*Publishers* Australia Pty Limited
ABN 36 009 913 517
www.harpercollins.com.au

HarperCollins*Publishers*
25 Ryde Road, Pymble, Sydney, NSW 2073, Australia
31 View Road, Glenfield, Auckland 10, New Zealand
1–A, Hamilton House, Connaught Place, New Delhi – 110 001, India
77–85 Fulham Palace Road, London, W6 8JB, United Kingdom
2 Bloor Street East, 20th floor, Toronto, Ontario M4W 1A8, Canada
10 East 53rd Street, New York NY 10022, USA

National Library of Australia Cataloguing-in-Publication data:

Taylor, Henrietta.
  Lavender and linen.
  ISBN: 978 0 7322 8147 2.
  1. Taylor, Henrietta. 2. Taylor, Henrietta – Family.
  3. Businesswomen – France – Provence – Biography.
  4. Australians – France – Provence – Biography.
  5. Tourism – France – Provence. I. Title.
338.76092

Cover design by Louise McGeachie
Cover image by Chris Sanders/Getty Images
Typeset in Bembo 11.5/16pt by Kirby Jones
Printed and bound in Australia by Griffin Press
79gsm Bulky Paperback used by HarperCollins*Publishers* is a natural, recyclable
product made from wood grown in a combination of sustainable plantation
and regrowth forests. It also contains up to a 20% portion of recycled fibre. The
manufacturing processes conform to the environmental regulations in
Tasmania, the place of manufacture.

6 5 4 3 2 1   08 09 10 11

On This Side in France

To Claire Larmenier,
who holds my head above the chaos that surrounds my life —
usually of my own making.

To Mimi and Harry Taylor,
who continue to love and support their errant and wayward
mother.

To my friends and neighbours in St Saturnin les Apt —
you light up my life.

Je vous aime tous.

CHAPTER ONE

Home Is Where the Heart Is

Christmas 2001

By the end of November, the temperature in sunny Provence suddenly shoots downwards. Perfect one day and even better the next becomes the exact opposite, and the inhabitants go about their business of preparing to hibernate for the next three to four months, taking cover from the arctic winds which sweep across the fields, rattling windows and shaking doors. Christmas decorations are brought out early to convince shoppers that there is good cheer aplenty. Songs about sleigh bells, jingle bells, White Christmas, snowballs, reindeer, snow and frost ring out across the airwaves.

We had been living in the south of France for eleven months and still could not extricate ourselves from dreams of crashing surf, sunburn, spicy Asian food, mangoes and cherries and the cricket. Yet the bronchial dilator, along with a year's supply of Ventolin capsules to ease the children's chronic asthma attacks, never saw the light of day; every month they were pushed further into the depths of the bathroom cupboard. There are air-quality tests taken annually in the Luberon that prove that it continues to have the least pollen and pollution in France. This dry, pollen-free climate had been an unexpected bonus for our health. The remarkable physical change in both Mimi and Harry was not a factor I could overlook lightly. At a family meeting, we had decided that we would stay in France for three years and then reassess the situation. These family meetings were held almost nightly, and our assessment of our position changed dramatically in line with the type of day we had had. The very fact that I repeated as a daily mantra that we had an achievable three-year goal that we were working towards — as a team, I dared to add — made the children believe that I actually had a firm grasp on our family's destiny. Always trying to show both sides of the argument, I pointed out that it was also essential in life to remain totally flexible. This was really an escape hatch that I had built into my argument, because the reality was that I had very little idea what I was doing and I was quite prepared to throw in the towel the moment the going became too rough.

Even with our three-year plan, we needed a quick trip back to Sydney at Christmas time for a break from all things French. The French, after all, were just too French! We were three Australians who still called Australia home.

Apart from sitting almost perfectly still in the same seat in a flying metal tube for over twenty-four hours, the long flight from France to Australia was effortless. There was absolutely nothing I could do to resolve all the tricky questions that had been playing on a continuous loop in my mind during those twenty-four hours. Even I wasn't particularly sure why I had chosen to take my children and live in the south of France; on a different continent — not even in the same hemisphere. During this visit our friends and family in Australia would be asking why we were living there and how long we were staying. The answers were somewhere in my befuddled mind. Somehow I had to convince everyone that I knew exactly what I was doing, even though I could see gaping holes in my logic. Friends would say behind my back that grief from my bereavement, nearly six years previously, as well as excess alcohol, had finally taken a firm grip on my reasoning. Maybe they would be right; but at the time we moved to France, I had never felt surer about anything.

The years before the move had been a roller-coaster ride of grief, pain and struggle. My beloved husband Norman died in 1995 after a terrible struggle with cancer, leaving me a single mother of two young children with only bittersweet memories of our happy life BC (before cancer) for comfort. A black hole of grief and alcohol swallowed me up, from which I finally emerged thanks to the staunch support of family and friends. Including, strangely enough, Latin Ray — former lover, former high-flying businessman, always besotted with Latin (hence known variously as Latin Ray or the Latin Lover). Just as I was coming up for air and starting to make a life and a home in Sydney for our family, my mother Sheilagh died and it was clear that a new era was beckoning. A six-month break in another country seemed just what Mimi, Harry and I needed — and so we came to the medieval *village perché* of Saignon, teetering above the busy market town of Apt in the heartland of Provence. Before I knew it I was forging a new life as the proprietor of three houses — two holiday rental properties in Saignon, and another house for us to live in, near the village of St Saturnin les Apt — making friends, making mistakes (lots of them) and learning the unwritten rules of life in a small French town. Bubbling away in my head now were a host of questions, with one big one leading the way:

1. *How can Raymond and I have a relationship across two continents?*
2. *Are we doing the right thing, living in France?*
3. *Will we make money out of our properties or will they drive us to penury (and me to drink)?*

Mimi and Harry were now seasoned travellers so they had been able to sleep most of the way, whereas I always found that long-distance travel gave me time to mull over problems and decisions, which inevitably led me to drown my thoughts in far too many combinations of exotic alcoholic beverages, aspirins and the dubious congealed food in small foil packages that was available to bored travellers on demand during the course of the voyage. My legs were encased from the knees down in surgically approved elastic stockings that had apparently cut off all blood supply to my lower limbs, in an effort to avoid deep vein thrombosis. Underwear had rubbed red welts into my skin, which was dry and papery from dehydration. A long hot shower was the only remedy for my aching body and overactive mind, followed by the prerequisite pots of tea and toast that would be waiting at my father's home. Everything else would have to wait.

I hummed festive carols about a white Christmas, sleigh bells and peace on earth and thought happy thoughts of toast and tea, but they vapourised instantly when a customs officer put a hand on my shoulder and asked me to come with him to have my bags inspected. A small piece of tinsel holly was tucked discreetly into a buttonhole in his shirt pocket but the welcoming smile was missing. Don't make a scene, my children mouthed to me silently. At the ages of almost eight and ten respectively, Harry and Mimi understood the workings of officialdom and they knew only too well my ability to cause a fracas. I struggled to keep my mouth tightly shut and my views to myself. Offending items were taken out of my bag and waved under my nose: Belgian chocolate Christmas decorations. The felonious baubles had been sighted and duly noted as they passed through one of the many X-rays that scanned vigorously for food, plants and seeds in an effort to keep contagious diseases away from the pristine Australian shores. The label stated in numerous languages that they were Christmas bells; however, on the flickering grey X-ray screen they resembled misshapen hand grenades. After the terrorist attack on New York's World Trade Center three months previously, nothing was being left to chance. The expensive chocolates were left in the safe hands of the customs inspector and we were free to wheel our remaining luggage into the arrival lounge and into the arms of our family. Mimi and Harry began to sneeze, cough and wheeze. Their little shoulders took on that all too familiar hunched-up look that signalled the beginnings of asthma attacks.

The children dragged themselves off into various parts of their grandfather's home for a short recuperative nap before the first round of family visits, which had been scheduled for lunchtime. The urge to swim in the salty sea and feel the sun on my skin outweighed the desperate tiredness that was sweeping over me in spasmodic waves. Experienced travellers are divided in their opinions of the best way to combat severe jet lag, but having travelled extensively from a young age, I always attempt to exercise as soon as possible after a long trip. Swimming or diving through pounding surf usually washes away the cobwebs and temporarily gives me the impression of having beaten the dreaded jet lag — until it king hits me in the late afternoon.

Carefully avoiding the glance that I knew was coming my way, I asked for the keys to my father's car to drive across the Spit Bridge and into Manly — its surf beach was second only in reputation to the internationally renowned Bondi Beach on the other side of the harbour. Manly was also the home of my Latin Lover. Sex, sun and surf: I wanted all three but found that even at forty-three years of age, it was difficult to admit this to my father. With the keys in my hand, I did not wait for the lecture about jet lag and driving, let alone the suggestion that I might be over the limit at nine o'clock in the morning after twenty-four hours of nonstop drinking. I fobbed off my father's questions about who I might see in Manly. The children were fast asleep. The dreaded asthma attacks had been avoided but the watery eyes and running noses had started as the polluted pollen-laden Sydney air rushed into their lungs. For a short time I was free. The lure of Manly was just too strong. During the trip I had memorised my list of urgent things to do first:

1. *Have a shower.*
2. *Speak to my sister Kate and her family.*
3. *Organise when and where to meet them on Christmas Day.*
4. *Organise the Christmas festivities.*
5. *Buy a well-fitting bra.*
6. *Avoid speaking to Raymond.*
7. *Avoid having sex with Raymond.*
8. *Break up with Raymond.*

It wouldn't have taken a genius to work out the fundamental flaw in my relationship with Raymond, my Latin Lover, my Mr Darcy, my first true love, whom I had met when I was twenty-two and impressionable. Destiny and my parents' influence had pulled us apart. But much to my father's horror, Raymond had come back into my life.

Raymond had come, at my insistence and for the first time, to live full-time with us in France from January to October 2001. His job was to offer me physical and emotional support while I started up my holiday rental business. I also desperately hoped that he would be able to show me how to set up the financial side of a small business, as that was his line of expertise but it was something completely alien to me. As a side issue, I expected him to fall thoroughly and hopelessly in love with me and never want to leave my side because the veil of confusion would finally be lifted from his eyes, enabling him to make wonderful vows (similar to marital ones) of dedication, commitment and loyalty.

It wasn't as though I had asked him to join me in the depths of the Amazon jungle or in the deserts of North Africa. Our new French home was in the prettiest part of the Luberon Valley, sixty kilometres east of Avignon and about the same distance from Aix-en-Provence. We were surrounded by endless vineyards, cherry orchards and olive trees that stretched gloriously across the countryside. Every month there was an extraordinary change in the landscape; the purple irises on the side of the roads in April followed by the profusion of red poppies in May made most people's jaws drop. But nothing ever compares to the simple beauty of fields of waving lavender stretching in long straight lines across the rolling hills or the sunflowers that take over in late July. Many men would have killed for a short sabbatical from life in these surroundings with no strings attached.

Our fairly average household consisted of one bereaved widow, two children and two recent additions, our kittens Sootie and Tiger. I doubted whether it was the kittens that had tipped the scales to make life unbearable. To be fair, Raymond had said from the beginning that he would never stay in France and live with us forever. Deliberately, I put his words out of my mind for ten months, knowing that the power of true love and the beauty of Provence would eventually win him over. But it had not. And now I was in the process of reassessing True Love.

Raymond now lived in Manly, whereas I remained steadfastly with my children in France. We were more than geographically challenged. But as I now lay in the twisted sheets of his bed and tried to fit together the pieces of my puzzle, to the best of my ability, I could feel myself sliding down the slippery path of total intoxication with this man and it had nothing to do with the fabulous bottle of French champagne that he had plied me with the moment I walked through the door.

Within one hour of landing in Sydney, I had lied to my father. Yet again I had lied to myself as I made a detour to Raymond's bed rather than heading for the beach: so much for my swim. Over the previous twenty-four hours — and the six weeks since Raymond left our home in France — I had come to the hard decision that it would be best if we went our separate ways. Passionate lovemaking and alcohol had once again weakened my resolve. Yet again I would need to reconsider my position.

How could our relationship survive the distance? Casual friends said that absence makes the heart grow fonder, whereas my closest friends repeated the old adage of out of sight, out of mind. We were attempting the impossible: keeping the flame of love alive across two continents, two hemispheres and a ten-hour time difference. Yet for the past six weeks of his absence, I had thought of nothing else. My life was completely and utterly out of balance.

Barely six weeks previously, outside the departure gates at Vienna airport, with a smile that split his crooked face in two, Raymond had pressed me to his lips and told me that he loved me and that we would visit each other at least three or four times a year. Good lying on his part, wishful thinking on mine. But then he had positively bounded through the sliding doors towards the plane that was Australia-bound. His tour of duty was over and he was heading home to surf, sun and cold beer. There had been times when he had actually enjoyed France, but the joy of carrying the morning baguette under his arm with a black beret on his head did nothing to assuage the discomfort he felt overall at being in France.

Manly, with its beautiful surf beach, was the best place on earth for him. France didn't even come in second. He couldn't wait to swim in the Pacific Ocean, feel the warm yellow sand between his toes, and drink cold Australian beer at the Steyne Hotel in Manly on Saturday mornings with his mates (all with widening girths) while their wives — if they still had them — went out to do the weekly shopping. We would just have to see how it worked out. Raymond believed that the hurdles would be small. We agreed not to discuss the future and to let it take care of itself; it was pointless to talk about it in any case, as there was very little room to compromise. All of these dismal, negative thoughts evaporated when Raymond reeled me into his arms yet again. After an absence of six weeks, he knew how to make a woman feel special. He loved me, he repeated insistently, and that was all we needed to make things right.

~~

The two weeks at Christmas were spent with friends and family by the beach, swimming, overindulging, laughing and drinking, playing tennis and reading books. Periodically, I wished that I could turn the clock back and that I had never left Sydney. My whole life had revolved around Sydney, my late husband Norman and my children. We were blessed with a wonderful extended family, including an assortment of aunts and uncles and cousins. After my husband's death, time did heal a certain amount of grief but a catchphrase continued to haunt my days and nights: life is so very short. Don't waste a precious minute. Destiny stepped in and the children and I found ourselves struggling through the middle of a horrendous European winter against the backdrop of the stark beauty of Saignon and surrounds. It was here that I learnt about life — or rather what constituted the essentials for my family and me.

As the temperature spiralled upwards during our Sydney holiday, so too did the pastiche of thoughts that whirled around unrestrained in my mind about the past few tumultuous years. Memories surfaced of the death of my husband, the ongoing saga of our financial affairs that was finally resolved in the Supreme Court, my alienation from Norman's family, my mother's death, and buying a new family home in Sydney only to discover that in fact France would become our home. My preferred European address had always been more along the lines of a wonderful villa among the cypress trees on the rolling blue-green hills of Tuscany, but this had not come to pass. Instead, for better or worse, we launched ourselves into a new life among the sixty-five million inhabitants of France. The linchpin of my success had been my incredible good fortune on the Sydney Stock Exchange, which had allowed me to buy three small properties in the south of France. Our lives spun around on an axis, hurtling us into a three- to five-year financial plan that was formulated and changed on a daily basis.

The aim of our Australian holiday had been to see family and friends, in particular Latin Ray, while also saying goodbye to our old lifestyle and loosening some of our remaining ties in Sydney. And this included Raymond. Yet no matter how many times I broached the subject with Raymond during our brief holiday, I couldn't bring myself to say that it was all over between us. As our time in Sydney drew to a close, I reasoned that I could move forward in our new life in France while things continued to be unresolved between us. The small impediment was that I still loved him.

~~

Arriving at the international airport in Roissy in the northeast outskirts of Paris plunged us all into bleak despair. We sniffled and coughed, pretending that we had caught colds from the air conditioning on the plane, but the harsh reality was that it was simply six o'clock on a freezing winter's morning in January. We were back in France, but this time we would be completely alone. 2002 was going to be a fresh new beginning. We had to learn to fend for ourselves, starting with catching the TGV train to Avignon and making sure that our entire luggage arrived with us. The winter mist rolled back as we sped past open fields and rolling hills, and the occasional cow or sheep lolling in the pastures. The train picked up speed and the signs on the roads running parallel to the track became blurred. Due to my secret tears and the speed of the train, I couldn't read any of the signs to see how close we were to Avignon, but the sudden appearance of an iridescent blue sky told me all that I needed to know; we were in the south of France.

Coming home after any holiday is difficult, but it's even more so when the holiday has exceeded all expectations. Mimi and Harry had spent most of their holiday shuttling happily between their cousins, aunts and uncles and grandfather. They had worked their way through all sorts of Asian food, traditional Aussie cuisine — pies with sauce, pavlova, barbecues — and their favourite: seafood. Chinese beef with black bean sauce and fresh sushi would be hard to find in the French countryside. They had watched every latest release VCR and DVD, lying in front of the blue flickering screen in a children's heaven at their Aunty Kate's home with half of the child population of Macmasters Beach along with their two older cousins, Jake and Hannah.

Our bags, a testament to our shopping expeditions, were bulging at the seams.

'Come on darlings, we're here. We're at Avignon.'

I tried really hard not to notice the tears streaming down Mimi's face, which was creased with fatigue and jet lag. 'Oh, *Maman,* I thought you said Avalon. Wouldn't it be nice to be in Avalon now? We could go and visit the Lucinis.'

Everyone was beyond tiredness but she was 100 per cent right: it would have been wonderful to be arriving at our friends' home near Avalon Beach for afternoon tea. Angie and I could idly pass the long afternoon chatting over endless cups of tea sucked through hard gingernut biscuits, while the children played indoors and out, slamming doors and whooping loudly with excitement as they all had when they were little.

Our trip from Sydney had taken more than twenty-four hours and then the TGV trip took three hours. I had my second wind and was feeling completely revitalised but I knew for a fact that my reflexes would be seriously dulled from fatigue. An extremely slow drive home was a necessity. Maybe this time the children would fall asleep during the fifty-minute drive to the house?

Being a single parent had taught me a few things:

1. *Try to be prepared for the unexpected.*
2. *Try to be prepared for the expected.*
3. *Just as one disaster is cleaned up, another will start.*
4. *Panic doesn't achieve anything.*
5. *Don't hesitate to ask for help.*

What if the car had been stolen or if the battery was dead and the motor did not start? A flat tyre would be the worst-case scenario. But my worries were for no reason. Our car was there, sitting in the same spot in the long-term car park, ready for action. It was really a miracle that we had all of our bags; Harry had spied my black computer case under the train seat just as we were leaving the compartment. I cajoled the children into the car and eased the gear stick into first, forgot about the clutch and promptly stalled the car at the gates of the parking area. We headed off cautiously down the main road, on to the RN100 towards Apt and then home to our house near St Saturnin les Apt. The drive along the RN100 is fast, straight and single carriageway for most of the way. There are large ditches on the shoulder of the road where you can still see the black skidmarks left by cars that have slammed on the brakes to avoid an accident with the car in front but ended up nose first in the ditch. Unfortunately, there are also too many ominous ceramic bouquets marking spots where some have been unlucky enough not to exit the ditch alive. The fields on either side of the road were dormant, the cherry trees denuded of leaves and the acres after acres of vines looking somewhat bleak and unloved, pruned back hard ready for the next season of foliage and fruit. It was such a stark contrast to the Sydney beachside landscape where we had spent the past seventeen days. But somehow, the winter-muted colours comforted my jaded senses. I had stepped into a watercolour painting that had a little too much water, and every colour blended into the next. Across the ochre-brown fields with the rich turned soil, up the unsealed track, past the neighbour's vines and suddenly we were home.

More than ever before, I knew that I had made the right decision. Home, we all sighed. *Ah, oui. Maison.*

CHAPTER TWO

Eggshell White

Our holiday had been a tremendous success in every way; all of our family and friends had believed my story that I had a foolproof and well-constructed plan for our financial triumph.

All of my life my mother had been able to see through my fibs. Since she had passed away, my father Jack was without help to decipher the shroud of half-truths and straight-out lies that bubbled over my lips. Now he believed wholeheartedly in what I was doing, and after seventeen days of saying the same thing, I actually began to believe it myself. Foolhardy and ignorant, I was attempting the impossible: beginning a business with no working knowledge in any shape or form about the basics of small business, in the face of an international downturn of the economy and a very jittery tourism sector. It was only after I had bought three properties midway through 2000 that I realised the enormity of the folly that I had embarked on. How

on earth was I going to find clients for short-term
holiday rentals? More importantly, who was going to
clean the houses? Who was going to wash the sheets
and iron the tablecloths? During 2001, our first full year
in business, I watched in horror as my lily-white hands
turned into rough red paws and I found out the answer
to those last two questions: me.

The Americans, who made up a large slice of the
market, were staying at home after the horrific attack in
New York in September 2001; travel to Provence was
now fairly low on the average tourist's list. The few
bookings that had been made for 2002 had been
cancelled and the harsh reality of how I was going to
pay for the mortgages was looming; bankruptcy
became a very real possibility in my second year of
business.

There was a small glimmer of hope. A small but
constant trickle of clients from the United Kingdom
who needed some respite from the cold in the more
temperate climate of the south of France had begun to
contact me. The weather reports in the United Kingdom
were relentlessly dismal, with snow flurries and low
depressions battering the coastline while we continued
to enjoy blue skies and empty villages. Prospective clients
from all parts of the United Kingdom were looking for a
short break away from their hideous damp climate.
Combined with the price war between the airlines that
serviced the south of France, this made a short break to

Provence a very feasible mid-term holiday. The little *village perché* of Saignon, just four kilometres from the world-famous market town of Apt, was exactly what the clients wanted.

Most clients were booking only as far ahead as Easter, but when the first smattering of enquiries for the summer break were followed by concrete bookings, I could see a tiny speck of blue at the end of a very long tunnel. Expenditure had to be kept on a short rein to stave off bankruptcy, which meant that I would continue to do the vast majority of work. My list of skills was becoming more and more impressive. I was becoming confident in a range of fields:

1. *Photography — taking photographs of the properties.*
2. *Advertising — designing and printing pamphlets to send out to prospective clients.*
3. *Internet — scouring advertising sites to find those that were free or at last cost-effective.*
4. *Accountancy — keeping figures of income and expenditure.*
5. *Stocktaking — keeping the properties well equipped.*
6. *Interior design — finding ways to change the look of the properties inexpensively.*
7. *Housekeeping — cleaning and making beds as quickly and efficiently as possible.*

8. *Household linen — stain removal, folding and ironing sheets became my speciality.*

9. *Budgeting — keeping spending to a bare minimum without overtly scrimping became an obsession.*

10. *DIY — house-painting became a hobby.*

New Year 2002 meant a new routine for everyone. Now that Raymond was living on a different continent in a different hemisphere in a different time zone, I had to do the early morning wake-up call and the children would trot off to school by themselves. The year before had been so hectic for me — getting the properties ready to rent out to clients — that Raymond had taken up the challenge and became a home duties non-parent. It didn't really matter that he wasn't their father and that his parenting skills were woeful; both Mimi and Harry often pointed out that his role was more along the lines of 'retarded older brother'. The morning trip to school had been his special time with the children without my interference. He had been ostracised by the other fathers dropping off their children when he had suggested that they adjourn to the nearby bar and have a beer at eight o'clock in the morning. Understandably, Raymond was seen to have a serious drinking problem. So rather than bonding with the fathers, Raymond put energy into the children. During this time together, Mimi and Harry learnt to wolf whistle, spit cherry stones along the road, and most importantly, spit long and far while avoiding spittle on the chin. This would serve them better than the tricks I could show them: how to iron tea towels correctly and how to ensure that the shower curtain remained mould-free.

A 2002 calendar was put up in the kitchen, featuring typical Provençal sites, with school holidays circled heavily in red ink. The children were beginning to understand that another trip back to Australia was out of the question for the best part of a year. Raymond was following his dream of studying Latin as a mature-age student at Sydney University and was planning to visit us in late June, during the four-week break between semesters. I was cursing myself for my inability to break up with him at Christmas. There was never a good time. I knew that our future did not include him beside me but I just couldn't bring myself to cut him out of my life.

Wrapped in layers and layers of thick sweaters and woolly scarves, huddling close to the fire that refused to blaze on a cold January night, we hibernated like everyone else and waited out yet another rigorous Provençal winter (though it was not as severe as the previous year). After our fantastic — if too short — Christmas holiday in heatwave conditions, returning to wintry France had sent us all spiralling into a deep depression. Our barren home in St Saturnin les Apt was devoid of any beauty or charm and, worse still, had pathetically inadequate heating. When the decision was taken to come and live in France, we were embarrassed with a choice of three properties: two small houses in Saignon and a larger one in St Saturnin les Apt. Saignon was where I had originally lived with the children when they were seven and nine, during the six-month holiday that changed our lives. It is not on many maps, but like so many places nowadays, Saignon has been forced to adopt an international flavour as people from all parts of the world take up part-time or full-time residency. Christine and Thierry from the *boulangerie* put their customers at ease with some English phrases dredged out of books, movies and often from titles from pop songs.

It was obvious why we would live in St Saturnin les Apt rather than in one of the two properties in Saignon:

1. *The garden was huge, sunny and incredibly tranquil.*
2. *There was a good selection of shops in the village.*
3. *The village shops were open all year.*
4. *The village faced due south and was sunny and reasonably protected from the harsh Mistral.*
5. *The village school was thriving and had a first-rate canteen.*

Once bitten, twice shy: I was coming to terms with
basic survival techniques. The previous year I had learnt
the hard way that the moment the mercury took the
tiniest dip, you made a mercy dash to the supermarket
to fight it out with your neighbours, who were also
stocking up on provisions like long-life milk, pasta, rice,
vegetables and meat for the freezer before being
snowed in. Around the house I stocked up on ten-kilo
bags of industrial salt to spread on the path to stop the
ice, and checked that the woodheap was piled up high
with the extra cubic metres of firewood that had been
ordered at the end of summer, avoiding the risk of
having to make do with the poor-quality 'green' wood
that gives off black clouds of smoke rather than heat.
The chimney had been swept and I listened to the
same lecture from the chimney sweep about how
burning pine cones was not good for the flue as the
resin sticks to the sides, increasing the fire hazard. The
pinecones might be hazardous, but when the fire
starters are still sitting on the supermarket shelves, they
guarantee a blazing fire every time. A stockpile had
been assiduously gathered and stacked into boxes in the
cellar and in the courtyard. The thick winter duvets had
been aired and put onto the beds, with blankets at the
ready for the nights when the mercury would plummet
below minus ten degrees; the garden had been pruned
and elegant winter plant sheets had been draped and
secured around the more fragile plants to protect them

from the frosts; thick mulch had been ordered from the agricultural supplier and applied liberally around the garden beds to help protect some of the roses and lavenders. Inside the house were towers of books that had been ordered, to be devoured during the long winter evenings.

Another chain of reactions was under way too, starting with a telephone call from Raymond. During the course of our conversation, I had managed to pull off a large section of the extremely ugly wallpaper in the hall. There was no stopping now; I had to continue. Like everything else in the house, the wallpaper had been put up meticulously and underneath the psychedelic colours was yet another layer of plain paper for the base. Removing it all was going to be a nightmare. The former owners had an eclectic collection of the worst wallpapers that had been produced in France in the late seventies, which they had married up with some very nasty brown floor tiles.

At first Mimi and Harry were positively delighted about my homemaking efforts and became stars at the school as all the local children wanted to visit and help in the removal of wallpaper. Discreetly at first and then boldly, they would write obscenities in French and English across the old wallpaper and then I encouraged them to rip large swaths of wallpaper from the wall.

Masses and masses of paper were collected and jammed down tightly into extra-large black plastic garden bags, then taken to the local tip in Apt, where the official recycling garbage inspector told me the news I could have done without: all paper had to be sorted according to type: plastic-coated wallpaper in one skip and paper in the other. An hour was spent sorting the bags at the side of the skips, to the great amusement of the inspector, who watched me grappling with metres of billowing wallpaper. I had finally ripped the hideous heavy wood and brass hall light from the ceiling and thrown it into the car, too, for a one-way trip to the tip. The garbage inspector asked me greedily if I really meant to throw away such a quality lamp; he surreptitiously placed his hand on it, waiting for my response, which would allow him possession. I graciously permitted him to call this icon of interior décor his own.

Making the most of the period when there were just the three of us, I had made an executive decision about the children and the canteen at school. It seemed silly that they should stay the entire day, from nine o'clock to four thirty in the afternoon four days per week and a half day on Saturday. It was far too long, in my opinion, especially when there was a long lunch break and we lived so very close to the primary school. More to the point, I really missed them. Since I was working nonstop at the house, it made sense to have a break with them and eat our main meal at lunchtime, like the French. I approached their teachers to see if I could take them out of school for their two-hour lunchtime. It transpired that their teachers had always been completely baffled by the fact that my children ate at the canteen when we lived so close by and especially since, as far as they could see, I did not work. It is crucial to the French and their culture to eat together at lunchtime. Step by step we were pushed into becoming more French.

So our family lunches began. The first few days I was constantly running late. Twelve o'clock came around so quickly. I would just get into cleaning and stripping wallpaper from room after room and it would be time to stop. As children came flying out of the school at midday, greeting their parents waiting patiently at the gate with three kisses on the cheeks, the teachers asked the two red-faced children remaining if it was a typical Australian habit or just a particularly quirky one of their mother's to leave them behind.

One day, they were taken away to ask the cook if two extra children could be fed. The canteen at the St Saturnin village school is renowned for the quality and variety of its menus. The cook has children begging for vegetables and dishes with Simone's Special Sauce that at home would not pass their lips. I arrived just as all the students were about to sit down at the many round tables in the canteen; the crunchy baguettes had been cut into manageable sizes for the little breadbaskets, and the salads, consisting of pieces of baby corn and cucumber and carrot sticks glistening with Simone's Special Salad Dressing, were in front of each place setting. I was in everyone's bad books with a black mark against my name but more was to come. Mimi and Harry looked aghast when they realised that I hadn't even bothered to buy the bread at the *boulangerie* at nine o'clock when I dropped them off at school, meaning that I would have to buy any type of baguette and be suitably grateful if there was any bread left at all. How could I be such an inadequate mother? I didn't have any time! I was rushing back to steam the wallpaper, a horrendous job that left hot sticky water in pools up and down the hallway in between the mounds of wet congealed paper. At least we could eat together in harmony, so I thought. At the table, we sat down with a glass of milk and a sandwich; both children raised their eyebrows in disgust at my plate of crunchy baguette with butter and Vegemite.

'*Maman*, what kind of lunch is this? Where is our entrée? We are used to having a nice little salad with fantastic dressing, isn't that right, Mims? We always have a hot meal of meat and vegetables followed by a good selection of cheeses and some fruit. And everyone knows that you don't serve milk at lunchtime if there is some cheese, otherwise you are overloading in the dairy department. This is not a balanced meal.'

Mimi chimed in, barely letting Harry pause for a breath. '*Maman*, pick your game up or we are going

back to eat at the canteen and you can have your
horrid sandwich by yourself.'

I knew immediately that my genes had bypassed my
children and that their grandmother's genes and character
had manifested in them. They both made me feel
pathetic and not at all worthy to be their mother: I would
have to pick my game up, as they said. I had to try harder.

~~

It was clear during the first few weeks without
Raymond that a major decision affecting our lifestyle
had to be taken. Would I take the easy road and join the
expatriate community and spend my days talking to
semi-retired couples about the intricacies of living in
France, joining the canasta group, the walking group or
the drinking at the bar on Saturday group? There was
even a small core of Australians who lived part-time in
the Luberon, with a few putting down roots
permanently. Deirdre and Geoff lived in the
neighbouring village of Roussillon and were in the
throes of a full renovation of their home. Kit was tall and
rangy and good-looking, with piercing blue eyes. He
wore R.M. Williams boots and jeans and always took
pride of place beside any barbecue that was going, beer
in hand and joke at the ready. Although Kit was nearing
his sixtieth birthday, he still had a hell-raising side that
was definitely alive and well. Kit worked for a company

based in Amsterdam that dealt with international gaming laws in casinos, giving seminars all over Europe, and more recently spending a great deal of time instructing the burgeoning markets of Eastern European countries. Due to his peculiar work demands, Kit divided his life between Sydney, Amsterdam and the tiny village of Saignon, where he had created the perfect bachelor's palace of dreams. Kit came from Manly and knew many of Raymond's friends, and drank at the same bars in Manly. Although he had a heartbeat and was without walking canes, I had no intention of joining the queue to have a dalliance with him. All of the English-speaking community had a wealth of information about living, renovating and surviving the tsunami of paperwork required in France, but they were at a completely different stage of life to me. I certainly did not want to join — or be the subject of — weekly gossip sessions at the bar. It was a safe move to be friendly but distant to the English-speaking community.

If you listen to parents at the school fence, you can solve most of the problems of the world; my biggest problem was home renovating on a minuscule budget. Not for the first time in my life, I started by asking questions — lots of them. My new school acquaintances just rolled their eyes and licked their lips, as there is nothing a Provençal woman likes better than to hand out advice. They are proficient and resourceful in a wide range of subjects, particularly:

1. *Work.*
2. *Husbands.*
3. *Cures and remedies for childhood illnesses.*
4. *Fabulous Provençal dishes on a budget.*

As far as they could see, I did not work and had no husband, so we were restricted to the last two subjects, which they attacked with gusto.

'*Ah oui, bien sûr,* you English do not know how to cook with fresh vegetables or good-quality meat like we have here in Provence.' Already the advice was faltering on the starting blocks. In Australia we have an abundance of every type of fruit and vegetable, fresh herbs and Asian greens — and we don't have zee Mad Cow disease! But I was forced to think all of these things rather than utter a word aloud because on one crucial matter they were right: I didn't know how they ate a big main meal at lunchtime and still remained so svelte. This was one topic that was assiduously avoided. No Frenchwoman ever discusses her slimming secrets.

The next few family lunches were slightly more successful, though the children were unable to hold back the comment that there were no *féculents* to accompany the roast beef I had slaved over all morning.

'Well, Harry, what would you call a *féculent,* anyway?' Harry looked at me blankly, as though I had gone completely and utterly stark raving mad.

'What did you ever learn at dinosaur school? You know, things like white beans, lentils, red beans, chickpeas; I don't know what you call them in English but the list is endless. Anyway, a nice little lentil salad is what we eat at the canteen to go with a hearty beef dish.' I was now spending more time in the kitchen whipping up little culinary delicacies for my darlings than progressing with the wallpaper stripping.

Eventually, the walls were totally denuded and prepared for the first onslaught of paint. I thought that it would be easy to buy some paint and start the job. Of course, I was wrong. The other passion close to a Frenchwoman's heart is giving advice on home maintenance. They know the best brands of paint, the best techniques for applying paint, where to buy the said brand of paint for the best price. I nodded in agreement as my eyes glazed over. I had learnt at an early age that it is always best to agree with everything and then do as you please.

During the frenetic period of buying the houses in Saignon, it had been suggested that I should meet Monsieur Daniel Perrard, a clever man who dealt with financial planning, who could perhaps iron out some of the looming problems heading my way — things much like the iceberg in the path of the Titanic. I had discovered the previous year that his office staff also had some tremendous hints when it came to renovations.

Monsieur Perrard had an office in Apt, ideally situated next door to Bricomarché, a DIY supermarket, where I had already spent hours the year before searching for the perfect colour blue to paint the shutters at Rose Cottage, one of our Saignon houses, so that it wouldn't provoke the ire of the village people. An hour or two could be spent with Monsieur Perrard discussing French tax, budgets and my latest difficulties coming to terms with French life, and then the rest of the morning could be passed just thirty metres away in the handyman shop, sourcing all of my requirements for an afternoon's work with the paintbrush.

Valérie, an incredibly skilled and adept young woman, was in charge of Monsieur Perrard's office management and was also systematically advancing through the preparations for her forthcoming September wedding. Nothing fazed Valérie as she, too, spent what seemed like hours when Monsieur Perrard was unavailable explaining to me some foible of the French system that I was not coming to terms with: the opening and closing hours of shops, the French health system, the French taxation system, France Telecom, local councils. Every week I would arrive waving a ream of accounts or forms that had to be urgently filled in and completed, along with a board splattered with paint samples. She would calmly look through my papers, putting them into priority order — most went into the garbage bin. As she shook her head in disapproval of my paint colours, I, too, couldn't resist offering advice on wedding dresses and colour schemes. Finally, after buying brushes, along with matt, low-sheen and high-gloss paint across the entire colour spectrum, the family council decided in peace and tranquillity in front of the bare walls: eggshell white.

The painting was keeping me beyond busy. I could barely breathe. There was no chance of missing Raymond and the so-called perfect life I had given up in Sydney, or time to think about how my life was unfolding. My thoughts were in a neutral holding pattern — and it was not a bad feeling for a change. Amid the chaos that followed me constantly, a funny irregular rhythm of harmony was emerging. The children seemed to be positively thriving in our unusual life.

~~~

The first stage of the interior work was almost done. It was time to begin the work in the garden. The gardener had installed the watering system and hardy plants had been chosen at the local nursery, though the gardener gave a snort of derision when 100 blue and white agapanthus were put next to our truck.

'They will never grow in the microclimate of St Saturnin les Apt, *madame*.' Commonsense tells you that the locals know what kind of plants will flourish and which will suffer long and painful deaths. Once again,

my heart ruled my head and I insisted that a garden full
of bobbing white and blue pompoms waving on top of
tall stems was just the thing for me. I made a mental
note that on my next visit to Monsieur Perrard's office
I should ask if their competency ran to gardening
advice. A compromise was found and I bought twenty
agapanthus as a trial. The gardener loaded the pots into
the truck, along with masses of lavender and rosemary
bushes, standard and climbing roses and a whole range
of Provençal shrubs and trees that needed next to no
water — guaranteed to survive the harshest summer.
The gardener was right about the microclimate of St
Saturnin: it is completely unsuitable for agapanthus. In
the subsequent years, I discovered that they managed to
survive but they certainly did not flourish.

Less than three months later, the ugly duckling was
no longer ugly, though nor was she a raving beauty.
Our house would never have the old-world charm of
the two Saignon houses, but there was a lot to be said
for a huge sunny private garden and no stairs. The
white roses were already in full bloom and threatening
to take over a large section of the garden, as were the
pink ballerina flowers in little pots that had been
thrown in the back of the truck as a giveaway. The
ballerinas had gone forth and multiplied in profusion.
My fingers were crossed for the health of the
agapanthus because we had decided to rename the
house Villa Agapanthe.

Wandering through the house late at night while the children were tucked up in bed in their freshly painted rooms, relief flooded through me that I had finally kissed goodbye to that hideous brown paper, the beige stripes and the psychedelic blue and brown flowered paper in the main bedroom. There was still something missing. I couldn't quite put my finger on it until Harry was reminiscing about the bedroom in Sydney that he had had as a baby; he just loved all of my drawings of fish and mermaids on the walls. Poster paint and a small palette were bought from the art supply shop and I decided to draw and stencil ivy, grapevines, lavender and wisteria, making a colour theme in each bedroom.

Claire, a Frenchwoman whom I had met at one of the end-of-year school functions the year before, occasionally helped out my neighbour Pierre — a recent widower with three sons still at home. Nine-year-old Benjamin was in Harry's class at school, as was Raphaël, Claire's son. Pierre was struggling to keep his two older sons in line and was eternally grateful when Claire popped in with a cooked meal or to help out with some light housework. She was always arriving or leaving with armfuls of torn jeans and shirts that the three boys had managed to ruin during the course of their day. It didn't surprise me that she would be an excellent seamstress. She was whippet thin, always on the move, putting on a load of washing, doing a quick basket of ironing and rearranging the kitchen so that when Pierre came home at night it looked like the fairies had visited. On one of her visits to their house, I watched as she leant perilously out of a window, cleaning and polishing the tiny panes. Apparently her curiosity had also been piqued: what was the mad Australian doing with so much paint? Paint that, even from a distance, she could tell was incorrect according to her years of experience and Frenchwoman's know-how.

Invited down from her high perch, Claire arrived at the back door ready to give an appraisal of my paintwork. She gave me a ten-minute diatribe on how she could have transformed the house for very little expense due to her limitless expertise. Admittedly, all of her comments were valid, but I was not accustomed to anyone querying my work methods. The children and Raymond knew that I was never wrong. Claire was the sort of person who rubbed me up the wrong way. She rushed out of the house and I breathed a sigh of relief; she was a very bossy and forthright person, whose company was irritating and infuriating. My first impressions of her had been correct; she was incredibly generous and kind but far too domineering and strong. I was very glad when she returned to her window cleaning, leaving me in peace and quiet. The kettle was whistling, a warning that the water was boiled but also a sign from above saying, 'Lock the doors. Take care. She's back!'

Claire returned brandishing her tape measure and small pocket note pad, ordering me to hold the measure and jot down numbers. I basically succumbed to all of her commands. We had to make a list of what needed to be done, starting with the top priorities of carpet removal and checking that the electrical circuits were up to standard. Given that her husband was an electrician, she would make sure that he was available to help. The punch line was that all the curtains and slip covers for the chairs and sofas should be re-done — and of course upholstery was her speciality.

Every comment on colour and design that she made was correct. In fact, she was accurate about everything, but that did not stop her being a very scary person. Thin and wiry and very scary. Made even more so the next day when she started to wield the pneumatic drill, blasting through the concrete walls to install the new curtain rods. And the day after, when she arrived to lay the carpet with Patrick, her husband. While he lifted and dragged the carpet, we ripped off the skirting boards and carried the beds and the rest of the furniture into the hallway. Somewhere during the day, I became Claire's assistant electrician, as that was yet another of her part-time professions. Somehow, we worked like a team forged together over many years. Instinctively I knew when to hand things to her, measure, drill and stand out of the way. Neither of us knew that a pattern for our friendship was now set for life.

CHAPTER THREE

The Wild Thyme Patch

It was time for a pause. My days had been eaten up with home decoration and nonstop painting, leaving little room for leisure time or friendships. Tired from the constant running around, it was time for a weekend break. A change of scenery would give me the lift I desperately needed. Porquerolles, a small island in the Mediterranean just off the coast of Toulon and fewer than ninety minutes away by car, was the perfect solution. Deirdre, one of the local Australians who was always on the move, knew what I would need and where to go on the island. She also reminded me to leave as early as possible to avoid the traffic. The moment school finished one Friday afternoon, the children and I piled into the car, the boot overflowing with food, fishing equipment, swimming things, bags of clothes and bottles of wine. We had enough equipment to cover all eventualities for the next forty-eight hours. Weaving in and out of the traffic like a demented mosquito through the thick congestion of Toulon during peak hour, the children cheered me on, knowing that there was the barest of margins to park the car in the little car park and catch the last ferry of the afternoon.

Porquerolles is a jewel undiscovered by foreign tourists. It is mainly frequented by French people who relish the luxury of the warm Mediterranean water and long sandy beaches, no cars and a vast variety of restaurants and accommodation for all budgets. Our little apartment was ideal for our needs: nothing luxurious, but clean and comfortable. Early the next morning we were at the port hooking up fishing lines ready to catch a couple of the fish that were tormenting the children, swimming in large schools under the surface of the crystal clear water. Within moments, Harry had caught his first fish. Jubilant from his fishing triumph, he was ready to conquer the next challenge on his list. At the ripe old age of eight-and-a-half he had decided that the time had come to learn to ride a bike successfully. Standing on his hands and juggling three oranges would have to wait a couple of years. The weekend continued to be a series of triumphant events, marred only by the slightly inclement weather. We cycled and hiked all over the island, enjoying long leisurely meals munching on steaming bowls of mussels and chips; wine was savoured and books were started but never finished. Forty-eight hours somehow stretched into what felt like a week. Rejuvenated, we headed home ready to make some plans about our life directions.

~~~

The next day, over our two-hour lunch and between courses, I called an urgent family meeting, pouring out some of my concerns to the children. I told them that it was time to reassess our life decisions; what I really meant was that I needed to reconfirm them. I had worked out early in their childhoods that it made more sense and probably would give rise to more harmony than discord within the family if I allowed other people to help in the decision-making process, namely Mimi and Harry. So Mimi and Harry sat at the table and called the meeting open.

My finances were completely tied up in the three properties, so that for the first time in my life I had no escape hatch. My heart told me that I had committed to a period of three years maximum, my head told me at least five years, and Monsieur Perrard had dared to whisper ten years — or fifteen for maximum returns. I knew that there was no way we could return to Sydney, and certainly not into Raymond's arms, but I needed affirmation that the children could cope. Fibs, if not bare-faced lies, sometimes have to be told. I had never actually mentioned to Mimi and Harry that we

were in Provence for a minimum of three years. Since
our return from Australia I had learnt a great deal more
about my financial standing, and it was obvious that
there was really no choice in the matter.

Snatches of songs about love dilemmas came rushing
through my brain and joined together in a new refrain
as I tapped the tablecloth with a fork:

Should we stay or should we go?
That is something I must know.
My life's complete with both in tow.
Should we stay and dance in France?

I tapped loudly, humming da das and dee dees in time
with the ditty that I had just made up.

'Oh, *Maman,* stop it. You will never be a poet or a
songwriter. Pick your game up. This is serious stuff. In
any case, the decision has already been made.' Mimi
addressed the meeting, saying that it was best if we
stayed for a couple of years to complete some of their
education in France — and probably even to the final
year of her schooling — on the strict proviso that we
holidayed as often as possible in Sydney with friends
and family. Harry and I nodded our heads in
agreement. We liked it when Mimi took charge of
meetings. It meant that they were short and sharp. She
wanted coaching in French and maths so that the
transition from primary to secondary school would be

drama-free. Yes. I nodded my head. Perhaps somebody from the primary school would know a retired teacher who was qualified to give junior coaching? The biggest potential problem had just fallen off the list. Their adaptation into the French education system had been slow and arduous. My wise friends had no idea when they said that children learn languages within three months. This might be true for children under five, but as they progress towards ten years of age, it is difficult and slow.

Mimi and Harry's first foray into French school life had been in Saignon, barely two years earlier. They joined in classes where the teacher and two bilingual boys communicated with them only in English. On our return to France in January 2001, the children once again started halfway through the school year in Saignon. In September of that year, after our move to St Saturnin les Apt, Mimi and Harry had started in a new school, without the luxury of bilingual support. It had been far from easy for either of them, and most days there were tears at bedtime about the stupid French and the stupid French language, but slowly they were both making small steps in the right direction. When they started to parrot the advertisements on the television, I realised that they were making real progress.

Now that the educational side of our problem was resolved, the next point in question was financial.

Although we had some bookings for the 2002 season, starting off in Easter, it was looking more and more likely that potential clients would be leaving their travel arrangements to the very last minute. The running costs for the two rental houses in Saignon continued to spiral ever upwards, and although our home in Sydney was rented out, the numbers never seemed to add up correctly at the end of each month. There was very little margin for error. The bottom line was that I needed the houses to be open all year around — with me doing most of the work. My occasional meetings with Monsieur Perrard had now become almost weekly as he tried to navigate me through my financial woes and the basic elements of accountancy. This was the man who told me when I first met him that the most beautiful word in the French language was 'deductible'. He loved a challenge and I presented him with a major one on a plate. 'Have no fear,' he said time and time again. 'Bankruptcy is not a word we use in this office. Only solutions surround problems; we have to work out which one suits you the best.' His eyes twinkled and, twirling his very French moustache into tight vertical points, he generously gave up his time to explain his latest proposition to ease the monthly financial haemorrhaging with the mortgage repayments.

Even without Monsieur Perrard's years of experience, I could work out the best solution: we had to sell one or possibly two properties or find a new unstoppable source of clients who wanted to visit every single week of the year. If I managed to sell during the spring, our financial losses might not be completely devastating, although Monsieur Perrard had severe doubts on this point. On the infrequent occasions when I went to the bar where the English-speaking community congregated every Saturday, the talk was always of how the 2002 season was shaping up to be the worst on record, and that it would not be long before the women would be working the streets of Apt. The very thought was ridiculous in the extreme, but the underlying fear remained: everyone was finding it difficult, if not impossible, to meet their financial obligations.

My trip down memory lane halted abruptly and I put up my hand to address the audience of two. I began slowly:

'This September, Mimi is going to start high school in Apt. Now that Raymond has gone, there are just the two small kittens and the three of us. This house is looking seriously cute; I think that I should sell it before we mess it up. In my opinion, we should move back to Place de la Fontaine [our original house in Saignon], as it is only four kilometres from the new high school in Apt. What do you think?'

The outcry was loud and unremitting. They loved their nice clean modern house with large airy rooms and a level garden — a potential playground for the two labradors they wanted. Saignon was fantastic, but all their friends now lived nearby and went to the village school of St Saturnin les Apt. In short, I was the cruellest mother in the world. The ensuing stony silence and the icy stares indicated that this idea was not in favour.

How could I have read my children so incorrectly? I assumed that they would jump at the chance to return to Saignon, with its thick cobbled stone streets and bubbling fountains and the mysterious moans and creaks of Place de la Fontaine. It was a romantic notion that I thought would appeal to them and at the same time be extremely sensible. The sale of the property in St Saturnin would bring some much-needed money back into the coffers and ease the monthly mortgage payments. I had tried but I was failing. I had to be wise and cut my losses before it really became a total catastrophe.

'*Maman,* you are so selfish and inconsiderate. We should call you *MoiMoi* rather than Mum. No wonder Raymond calls you his Gimme Girl behind your back and under his breath. It's always me me me! Life doesn't just revolve around you. You cannot do that to us. We have been abducted from our country. It has been hell living here while you paint every day and forget about things like food on the table! Harry and I like living here in St Sat. Our friends come here because we have such a great garden. We want a black labrador for

Christmas. Each! We are not moving back to Saignon. This meeting is closed. That is the end of the discussion.'

Yes. That went well, I thought, except the reference about being egocentric and a Gimme Girl — that really stung. I was so glad that we had a forum to air our views. But somehow I would have to bring them around and make them see reason.

I was not going to be dissuaded by obstreperous children; we would sell Villa Agapanthe as quickly as possible, then move back into Place de la Fontaine. Early June would be a good date, giving the children a new address to start their new school year in September. This would relieve the stress of the enormous monthly mortgage payments and I could get back to enjoying life and being a much happier person and mother. My days of running rental properties were coming to a rapid close, I thought.

Mimi, who was sulking, came with me to visit a couple of houses for sale in the neighbourhood to get an idea of how much our house was worth and what the competition was on the market. In France, selling and buying real estate is done in hushed tones with no garish billboards in front of the property. Agencies come to the owner asking what price they are after. It was necessary to see what was on the market around St Saturnin to gauge what sort of price would be realistically achievable and the strength of the competition.

After viewing several properties in the area it was evident that there was little on offer — most was overpriced and poor value — and the bottom line was that, without exception, every house needed major renovation just to make it habitable. 'Learn from your mistakes', another of my parents' mantras, was ringing in my ears. 'Make a decision and stick to it but never be scared to walk away.'

The decision had been made and nothing was going to make me change my mind. Even though a frantic spell of bookings had come in in recent weeks, selling was no longer urgent but inevitable. It was simply a question of when. Should we sell this year or wait until Easter of the following year? This was the question I was mulling over as we followed the car of yet another real estate agent along a narrow country track leading away from the village of St Saturnin les Apt. Few of the tracks have names, making it impossible to find addresses unless you have extremely good directions. I had specifically asked to see modern houses with gardens on level land of approximately 2000 square metres (which for the French countryside is a traditional block), close to the village, so that I could judge what else was on the market in the same class as Villa Agapanthe.

From a distance, we could see a circular turret looming up from the little stone cottage set in the midst of trees and flowering bushes. As we swung into the driveway of the house I could see that this house was not comparable with ours — yet again, a complete waste of time. Here was an odd-looking cottage sitting on a vast tract of land, almost a hectare; the land was almost five times larger than Villa Agapanthe. Large garden beds brimmed with roses, lavender and lavender-blue and deep violet-purple flowering butterfly bushes; the heavy green straps of clivia and finer ones of amaryllis were evident too. On the ground I could see the grey felted foliage of lamb's ears, fragrant clumps of thyme in attractive mats, with some ivy that had been recently cut back hard. There was one bed completely devoted to every colour of iris imaginable. Who cares if they are only magnificent for a couple of weeks each year? I made a mental note that for preference I like them in mixed flower borders so that the motley leaves are not so evident.

Stop. What was I thinking? I was not buying this property, so who cared how they used the irises! A fiscal comparison to Villa Agapanthe was the only thing that was important. Everything had to be clinically assessed and emotions completely disregarded. As my mother said, a house is only bricks and mortar: your home is in your heart; you carry it with you wherever you are. This was strictly business. I needed to see how this house, *La Farigoulette* (in English the Wild Thyme Patch), measured up against my beautifully painted Villa Agapanthe. Some calm reflection was needed, for a change. My viewpoint had shifted towards a purely business perspective based on a clearly thought-out financial plan. My head and not my heart would rule all of my transactions from now on.

Mimi was sitting beside me in the car, transfixed by the massive black pine tree in front of her. She was always desperate to climb high to the heavens, perhaps for closer contact with her departed father. She sat immobile. Mimi had been stuck by lightning. *Coup de foudre. Coup d'amour.* Thunderstruck. Lovestruck. Call it what you will, but she was taken.

'*Maman*, this is the best house ever! You just have to buy it! This is our home. We have finally found it. You clever, wonderful *Maman*. You have found our house. Come on, let's go and investigate. Then we'll go and get Harry.'

Véronique from the real estate agency was standing beside her oversized four-wheel drive vehicle, looking immaculate: tall and willowy, sunglasses perched on her head, with her perfect bob of blond hair falling in a straight curtain. She had checked her notes and was getting ready for the hard sell while I made a note to ask for her hairdresser's name.

The house was a rabbit warren of pokey little rooms that all interconnected: a house full of doors and corridors. Drab colours had been painted at random in the bathrooms, and the tiny bedrooms were made even more hideous by the unattractive wallpaper that in turn made the ugly floor tiles look even worse. It was a triumph of bad taste and a waste of precious living space. I had never seen so many little corridors with doors using up the small amount of valuable habitable space. Villa Agapanthe was looking like a palace in comparison. In fact, you couldn't compare the two houses. It was oranges and apples. They both had a roof and were situated in St Saturnin les Apt, and that is where the common link stopped. 'Who in their right mind would ever buy a property like this?' I sniggered to Véronique. She quickly pointed out the potential of the land size and the evident need to do some minor renovations to the interior of the house. That's when I fell over laughing.

'Surely you can see that the only thing that this house warrants is to be pulled down and rebuilt further back down there, away from the road. No, I disagree with you entirely. It doesn't warrant a total overhaul, it is evident it is not salvageable. This is a perfect example of the need to be ruthless with a bulldozer. I can see a new house further back down there, something really clean and streamlined that lets in the light and takes advantage of this wonderful block of land.'

As I continued my visit, my mind went into a wander of what I would do to the house and land. I knew that I could never face any sort of renovation again. Never again did I want to refurbish, paint, scrub or prepare surfaces. It was all over. Less was best; no more property.

Véronique tossed her blond bob and with total dedication to her craft, she steered me towards the exterior, which she assured me I would adore. And of course she was right — in that the house was dowdy and pokey, and the large garden was the complete opposite.

The garden was awe-inspiringly huge, with a small private forest, a little orchard of worm-eaten peach, pear and cherry trees, and a large enclosed secret garden behind the house that could be used for a vegetable garden or *potager*. Best of all were the fish ponds that were dotted through the unruly garden; the largest was the size of a swimming pool, with islands and a bridge. You could barely see the water for the profusion of water lilies that spread in large drifts across the pond. Occasionally you could see the water stir and the flick of a fin as one of the mega koi carp leapt out of the water, diving back under the cover of the green lily leaves. I wasn't sure whether my eyes were playing tricks on me, but they looked to be over seven kilos and at least thirty centimetres long. I rubbed my eyes just in case I had accidentally fallen through a shard of time and ended up in Monet's garden. It was more than brilliant. I was home.

CHAPTER FOUR

The Arrival of the Pocket Venus

I knew deep in my heart that the idea of buying the Wild Thyme Patch was a complete and utter folly. An urgent appointment with Monsieur Perrard was necessary.

Walking into his office, I was ready to listen to cool, objective reasoning supported by the financial pros and cons. As usual, I brought with me armfuls of folders showing the budgets for the year and the booking sheets with projected revenues for 2002. For no apparent reason there had been a buzz of activity, with streams of solid bookings coming in from all parts of the world for the oncoming season. My fantastic website was paying off and prospective clients were desperate to come to the Luberon. Pressing his hand into the small of my back, Daniel Perrard steered me out of his office and into the bar next door. He had learnt from the first days of our relationship that several strong short black coffees and many cigarettes helped to solve the puzzles I so often lay in his competent hands. The dictum he used to apply the brakes to so many of my schemes was trotted out: figures do not lie. He flexed his fingers and reached for the calculator, a pen and a ream of paper.

We spent the next couple of hours locked in fierce discussion about the economy, the state of Provençal tourism, projected revenues, advertising costs, running costs and the escalating property values in the Luberon. For every negative, I flipped through my files until I was able to come up with a counter argument. Pushing the cold reality of monthly payments to the furthest recesses of my mind, my total obsession with this house spurred me on to create a plan that would save me from complete and utter ruin. Due to the recent spate of solid bookings, my projected figures would more than cover the money necessary to pay the mortgages. My problem was how to convince Monsieur Perrard that a third property would be a bonus to my holiday rental business, not a liability. We would move out of Villa Agapanthe by June and the holidaymakers would move in almost the next week. Their rent would cover the mortgage payments on the Wild Thyme Patch. Sweat had now broken out across his forehead and he told me in no uncertain terms that what I was proposing was financial suicide and under no circumstances would he

give it his approval. Our business relationship had now
stretched over two years: strictly professional, the rules
of conduct never allowing us to bend the social norms
and call each other by our first names. It was difficult to
hide the huge admiration that we had for each other.
But his world of accountancy was one of caution,
restraint and moderation. He promised me that he
would visit the property later that day and I promised
him that I would take the time to give the problem
some more much-needed reflection over the next
forty-eight hours. As it turned out, both promises were
broken.

～～

I needed to speak to another adult. I was sure that he
wouldn't mind talking business to me in the middle of
the Australian night. Delirious from lack of sleep, Latin
Ray mumbled through his yawns and said that he was
very enthusiastic about my latest scheme but one
o'clock in the morning was not his best time.
Apologising for my impulsiveness, I promised him
faithfully that I would do nothing until his arrival in
mid-June for a month's holiday, and as we spoke, I
jiggled the real estate's business card that Véronique had
thrust into my hand the day before.

'Of course, my love. As if I would go and buy
something without giving it great thought. It is not as if

I am buying a pair of shoes. Yes. You are quite right that going slowly is the best method and no, I haven't got my fingers crossed. And yes, I have been keeping my books up to date like you showed me. I am not completely useless and stupid.'

He could be such a boring stick-in-the-mud. And of course I had my fingers crossed while I was talking to him, so I knew that fibbing didn't count as fibbing. Chances were he wouldn't even remember our conversation the next day. I wanted the Wild Thyme Patch for our home. The more Raymond said I should wait, the more I realised that there was only one option left to me. I would have to speak to Nathalie, my bank manager in Apt, who luckily was a personal friend. Unfortunately, even though she could tell me various ways to borrow money, manoeuvring around the fairly stiff rules that apply to bank loans, no advice was forthcoming on how to pay the monthly instalments.

Nathalie was a young woman with two children roughly the same age as mine. She came from the Champagne region of France but had recently moved to Provence after her marriage breakdown. She was still finding her way emotionally and we had had many a long dinner consuming too many bottles of red wine while she came to terms unsteadily with the reconstruction of her family life. But when it came to financial matters, she was clear and concise. Her fingers flew across the number pad of the calculator as she too,

like Monsieur Perrard the previous day, dissected my
financial affairs. Patiently she explained to me that only
four-fifths of my revenue from the holiday houses could
be taken into consideration, to allow for a margin of
error. The family home in Sydney was rented out and
that was bringing in some money, then there were some
small dividends from my investments. Nathalie
explained about icing a cake too thinly. I nodded in
silent agreement. Once again those in the know were
right and I was definitely wrong.

Having lived in Sydney throughout an extremely
aggressive property boom, I possessed a fairly distorted
and naïve view about real estate. My previous forays into
property had always been more about having incredible
good luck than possessing the astuteness to hunt for the
ultimate bargain; here in Provence, the bottom line was
that there were few barnyards or farmhouses to be had at
giveaway prices. The Wild Thyme Patch had a load of
positives: the size and location of the land dominated the
list. Granted, it was not a bargain but at the same time, it
was relatively good value and it would work perfectly for
my needs. The little house was not ideal, but that could
always be changed at a later date, when things became
more financially stable. The presiding factor was that if I
kept Villa Agapanthe rather than selling it, three rental
properties would add more scope and flexibility to my
business. In the short term, we would downsize our
family needs for the sake of the business. My heart had

ruled in the past three transactions, but on this occasion, I desperately tried to convince myself that it was my head that was ruling my actions.

Buying the Wild Thyme Patch made good economic sense in the long term but the short-term problem was tricky: how was I going to pay for it? Bridging finance interest rates were gruesomely high, and it would have been an act of utter recklessness to even entertain the idea. I had a small amount of money in reserve for real emergencies but not enough to put down a deposit on the house. It was purely academic how much the loan would cost. I simply couldn't afford the house at this price. It was time to speak to Véronique, half of the husband-and-wife team from St Saturnin les Apt Real Estate, to see if we could negotiate a price and a deal with the owners.

After hours of throwing figures into the calculator, Nathalie formulated an arrangement that was vaguely agreeable to me and very acceptable to the bank, so the deal was sewn up: I could buy the Wild Thyme Patch without resorting to my favoured alternative of selling one or both of the children. However, the bank now owned the children, the two cats, the four properties and me. On the positive side, we would make the Wild Thyme Patch our new home and live happily ever after.

~

All property transactions must come before a notary in France, whose title is *Maître* rather than the usual *Monsieur*. I felt slightly ill at ease when I discovered that *Maître* Jaffary, who had processed my previous transactions, was unavailable. Instead I would be dealing with his associate, the very capable Mademoiselle Pruvot. Her office was streamlined, neat and tidy, with few personal belongings in view — 100 per cent professional. While waiting for her to seek out the thick file of the transaction, I mulled over the problem about the French language and its obsession with correctness. Should I call her *Maître* to reflect her legal status or did one use the feminine word, *Maîtresse*? I had limited experience with problems such as this. At the children's primary school, the children addressed their primary school teachers in the masculine or feminine form, using *Maître* and *Maîtresse*. It did not make sense for me to address someone in the same way that a five-year-old would address their teacher. Such aspects of the complexity of the French language perplexed me on a daily basis.

My French vocabulary had increased spectacularly over the past year, living and working with tradesmen while renovating Rose Cottage. Now that Latin Ray — a firm non-French speaker — was living in Sydney and our circle of French acquaintances was growing, the percentage of time that I spoke French during the day was increasing rapidly. But there was still the old stumbling block of my cultural inadequacies. When you have a disability you learn how to disguise it or make light of it. My method was to wait until Mademoiselle Pruvot introduced herself and if she called me by my very formal name of *Veuve* Taylor — Widow Taylor — I would know that I should do likewise and call her *Maître,* thus establishing the culturally and socially correct gap that existed between us. You only get one chance to make a good first impression with the French. I would take my cue from her. She introduced everyone with their correct titles and used *vous*, the polite form of 'you'. For the next hour or so I would be *Veuve* Taylor and she would be addressed as *Maître.* Once the formalities had been dispensed with I could slip into the comfort zone of words and business dealings that were now familiar to me. Her choice of language indicated to me that she was extremely friendly but still highly professional — observing all the correctness that her profession warranted. The German vendors of the Wild Thyme Patch were finding the whole operation very stressful, mulling over every sentence as they struggled with all the nuances that were explained to them with dreary monotony in French, English and finally German. But at last the contract was signed and we could begin to pack our bags.

The exchange of contracts was negotiated for the beginning of the summer of 2002, just before the onslaught of the arriving visitors — Latin Ray, followed by various members of my family arriving from Australia in continuous waves throughout July and August. In the midst of the general chaos, I had several emails from Amanda Wood, a young Australian girl working in Switzerland who had stayed with her family at Place de la Fontaine in February. At the end of her idyllic week in Saignon, Amanda had been reluctantly preparing to return to her job as an au pair while her parents and sister headed back home to the sweltering heat of summer in Australia. I jumped straight in, offering her a position with me. I was in dire straits, with a complete lack of computer knowledge and skills in basic office administration tasks such as filing, photocopying and scanning documents. I needed a mother's help in the office, not with the children, who were almost autonomous. Amanda seemed competent and organised and had the computing and office skills I needed — and she was fluent in French. Looking abashed and somewhat embarrassed, she said that she would think about my fabulously underpaid job. I told myself that Amanda Wood would never be seen again.

I couldn't understand why she hadn't jumped at the chance, but maybe it was because she knew that winter would be unbearable in Villa Agapanthe due to the very limited heating. Four months later, in late spring, the weather was warming up, she was looking to move closer to the sea and her sights were firmly set on Provence, where she could work on a honey tan to enhance her lithe body. Thinking that we could help her achieve this, she contacted me. Why I agreed to allow her to come to stay on the cusp of summer was a mystery, as we were about to move and the onslaught of visitors was about to commence. The Wild Thyme Patch had three bedrooms and one bathroom. Pitching a tent in the enormous garden was becoming a serious option.

Amanda arrived one day at Avignon airport with a backpack larger than herself. I had dropped everything to go and pick her up from the airport. She slid into the passenger's seat of the car, leaving me to manoeuvre her overladen backpack into the boot. Already things did not augur well. As I negotiated my way around the other cars in the car park, I told her the one strict rule that I did not bend under any circumstance: no smoking anywhere near me, near the houses, near the children. No smoking meant no smoking. She blithely said that she did not smoke, but I noticed that her nicotine-stained fingers were crossed as she gazed out the window asking about the nightlife in the village. Actually, there is none, I told her. And that goes for our swimming pool, too. There isn't one. Amanda began the lip tremble: a trembling bottom lip perfected by my older sister Kate in her youth, designed to melt the hardest of any adult's heart to gain whatever she wanted

— but I looked purposefully ahead for oncoming kamikaze cars hurtling towards me along the straight and narrow single carriageway of the main road that cuts through the countryside in a straight line from Avignon to Apt. The wonderful, clever Amanda was going to help me with my problems with the computer and arrange my filing systems to make things work more efficiently, in between lying in the sun reading and cycling around the neighbourhood. I was deliriously happy. Finally someone would show me tricks about computers to make my life easier. What Amanda didn't know was how big a role I needed her to play during the three days after her arrival. There was the packing and unpacking of boxes for our move to the new house and the washing and ironing of sheets for the clients for Saturday. Summer was my busiest time with the properties, and the sheets and housekeeping still had to be done while all hell was breaking loose around us.

～

Early the following day Raymond arrived from Sydney via Paris. He had a vague notion that I hadn't taken his advice about the purchase of the house as I had told him that I had a really big surprise for him and he was learning from experience what that meant. The last time we spoke, he said that he was exhausted from his first term of studies and was desperate to get to France to enjoy sitting around with me under the shady trees as we had in the summer of the previous year. I wasn't about to shatter his illusions. I couldn't afford to let him change his mind so I decided that it was best to keep him — like Amanda — in the dark. It would be highly unlikely that any time would be devoted to sitting around doing nothing.

The big move into the Wild Thyme Patch took place a couple of days later, at the end of June, to coincide with the end of school. Harry and Mimi had been loudly voicing their opinion that it was time for a new television to replace the one that was slightly larger than the size of a postage stamp. Amanda offered to take me shopping for large-screen televisions.

Yet again, the issue of English television was raised. In the non-French community, many opt for English satellite television to be beamed into their homes, at great expense. At the back of my mind, I thought that if we had English satellite television and a larger screen, Raymond might be influenced to give up his studies in Australia and move to France in order to live with the children and me. Maybe even one day enrol in an English university where he could study Latin to his heart's content? If only I could find somewhere he could study nearby, he might want to stay.

That was if I decided that I wanted him in my life full-time. He was a man of basic needs: loads of sport on television, where they called the play in English not

French; cases of beer; roast chicken and lamb as often as possible, washed down with a palatable red; and — whenever the children were at school or out of hearing distance — a compliant woman, namely me. It revolted me that I could be so pathetic. Total and utter confusion reigned in my mind. I couldn't come to terms with the fact that one moment I was desperately in love with him and the next I wanted desperately to move on with my new life in France. The bribe of expensive English satellite television was to get him to stay with me for just a little longer so I could make up my mind.

Our neighbours, nine-year-old Benjamin and his family, had just left our street and moved to the village of Rustrel, seven kilometres away. I had placated Harry with the fact that Benji would be coming almost daily to swim in the public pool in our village so they would still remain friends. A week after their move, I dropped Benji off at their new home after the boys had been playing together after school. Fairy fingers had been at work. Objects, photographs and books lined the walls of their new living room, in the same controlled order as always. It was almost possible to think that a magic wand had been waved and everything had been transported to the new house without skipping a beat. I should have known that it was Claire who had organised the move; she had the whole thing taken care of before Pierre, Benji's father, even knew that it had happened. She was simply an extraordinary type of woman. Someone I could admire greatly from a distance — a very long distance. Boxes had been packed, labelled and put into the truck that Claire then drove to the new abode, where she unpacked and arranged everything in order. By the time that Pierre had finished work, all he had to do was to remember to drive to his new home.

As Claire's son Raphaël was in Harry's class, she had found out from the school grapevine that we, too, were about to move. Although I found her to be the bossiest and most overbearing person I had ever encountered in my life, I was secretly relieved the day that she presented her services to help with the move. At least I would have another adult able to help, as both Amanda and Raymond were lying under the trees in a state of exhaustion from waking up just before lunchtime. Mimi adored Amanda, seeing her as the older, clever sister she never had, and both children continued to consider Raymond as slightly mentally deficient. Lazy or stupid, it was irrelevant as at least they could both drive, which was a major asset. Claire arrived bearing large armfuls of cartons and thick brown tape with instructions for everyone about how to pack successfully. Both Raymond and Amanda jumped to attention and were given a list of directives for the day. It occurred to me that maybe Claire wasn't so bad after all. Amanda was placed in charge of packing boxes and proved to have a natural flair for wrapping, stacking and packing in a careful, orderly manner.

Somehow we managed to move the mountains of boxes from one end of the village to the other, to our new abode nestled in the outskirts of St Saturnin les Apt. Then Raymond and the children began the hideous job of unpacking and rearranging our life into shelves, cupboard and closets. Most of the boxes with my folders and important papers remained beside the desk waiting to be unpacked — much later. Claire issued the order that the priorities were to unpack the kitchen and make the beds. We hurried to comply. All the pieces fell into place when Claire mentioned that her first husband had been a military man and her second husband, Patrick, had been one too until recently. She had lost count of how many times she had moved the family's belongings. As twilight was falling she returned with Patrick and Raphaël, bearing a huge bottle of wine tucked under her arm. Her eyes twinkled with amusement as she watched Raymond rummaging through the boxes of kitchen equipment looking desperately for a corkscrew. 'Don't you know that we French always carry one in the glove box of our car?'

Everyone was in a state of exhaustion, lying supine under the shade of the large pine tree. Some clean glasses were fetched from a box and Raymond opened the bottles of red wine and apple cider to weak applause from us all. Moving is said to be one of the most stressful times in your life; in one day we had achieved the near impossible due to Amanda's incredibly methodical packing and with Claire and my family unpacking in the new house.

~~~

Amanda was installed in one of the attic bedrooms and the kids would soon join her upstairs in the other large space, which Claire and I had converted into a makeshift bedroom, anticipating the impending arrival of family members. Raymond was still suffering from jet lag and wanted to play up rather than get under the yoke and start unpacking boxes of books and clothes or even better, washing and ironing. He insisted that the work would still be there the next day and that we should unpack gradually so that everything would go into the correct place first time. After all, the television and the fridge were working, the beds were made; nothing else was urgent. It was time to go to the local bar. There, Amanda caused a sensation among the young males of Apt. Blond, petite and very cute, as only twenty-something girls can look in strappy barely-there summer clothes, Amanda's arrival whipped the local young men into a frenzy of testosterone.

Over the past two years, I had come to realise that I was far from being incapable and incompetent in all fields. With Amanda's help putting in order my computer and files and streamlining my various stabs at basic accounting, I would find the money to pay for the mortgages. Nothing would stand in my way. I was ready to pack away my poor weeping widow garb and replace it with my new guise of Wonder Woman, sleeves rolled up, wearing a crisp linen apron and bearing a cake of Marseille soap.

CHAPTER FIVE

The Long-term
Clients

The immediate and pressing challenge that lay ahead was
how to obtain clients for my latest rental property, Villa
Agapanthe, especially as nobody in the United
Kingdom, America, Canada, Australia or New Zealand
knew of my lovely holiday home's existence and now,
midway through the tourist season, it was far too late to
begin any sort of advertising in the print media. Most
clients booked well in advance, so the chances of
obtaining enough last-minute bookings were slim. This
third property would stand very little chance of bringing
in any sort of revenue, constant or otherwise, for the
2002 season. Nathalie, the bank manager in Apt, felt that
I was approaching serious over-extending and kept
repeating the 'too many eggs in one basket' mantra. After
our first meeting she had spelt it out clearly so that there
could be no misunderstanding:

1. *The three properties had to be taking in paying clients.*

2. *They had to be open all year round to obtain maximum capacity.*

3. *There was little to no room in the budget to pay for help with the cleaning, washing and ironing.*

4. *Inviting family members for free holidays did not help the budget.*

5. *Offers of 'mate's rates' had to be kept under control.*

6. *Costs had to be kept to a strict minimum.*

7. *I had to break up with Raymond, whom she found to be oafish and a bore.*

Nathalie and I concentrated solely on business matters when she was in office mode but as she was guiding me towards the exit, grabbing her handbag and a large clutch of keys, she mentioned the last item. I had wanted to discuss my financial problems over lunch — after all, it was lunchtime and the bank had to close — but obviously she thought otherwise.

~~~

I could not depend on chance telephone calls from the United Kingdom to fill up the booking sheet that was looking ominously empty. With Amanda's dexterity with the computer and her increasing technological expertise, it did not take her long to find a long list of Internet sites that either had a free ninety-day trial period or a low annual cost, so that we could add Villa Agapanthe to their lists and thus generate inquiries that could flow on to solid bookings. At the same time, Amanda was patiently showing me how to organise the bookings and revenues from Place de la Fontaine and Rose Cottage. For someone so young she was admirable in her capabilities; as the temperature rose dramatically she became cooler and less flustered by my series of inane questions.

The statement on the first massive payment for the four mortgages had arrived, sending me reeling back and making it extremely difficult to remain buoyant and positive. The clients were out there; I just did not know how to reach them. How could I send them a message about our wonderful countryside, which was improving daily? Provence did not get any better than this. The weather was idyllic; the days stretched endlessly with long hours of sunlight then fell dramatically into balmy still nights. The muted colours of winter had finally been replaced in late March with fields of cherry trees laden with white blooms, only to be upstaged in the subsequent months by the wonderful clumps of intense purple and white irises, and the red poppies along the roadside nestling below the bright yellow fields of canola. In July the fields of lavender intensified from pale mauve to a richer hue against green stalks, rippling in the breeze in perfect straight lines. So how could I get these images to my prospective clients, wallowing in their raincoats amid yet more summer rain?

Weekend papers with large travel sections in London, New York, Washington, Toronto and Amsterdam — even the Hollywood trade papers — were my next points of attack. With Amanda's help I worked out the rates for advertising and the possible attainable revenue. Prospective clients from the United Kingdom were waiting patiently to see if any last-minute airline deals could be got before committing themselves to a particular part of France. It appeared that most of the travellers were going to Spain, and then there was a large section of the tourist pie tempted by introductory deals to new venues such as the Dalmatian coast in Croatia.

~~~

Judging by my clients during the 2001 season, my clientele base would be mainly serious travellers, well read and well versed in everything concerning Provence. They had arrived with pages of photocopied notes or printed sheets from Internet sites spilling out of matching suitcases bursting with carefully chosen clothes. The clients also had a list of questions ready to throw at me the moment I indicated that I was available.

But from their months of research, they already knew the best restaurants, the best deals on hiring bikes, and where to go for kayaking, walks and picnics in the Luberon. Specific days had been set aside to visit the markets in the area; the cheese market in Banon, the breathtaking rose show in Simane la Rotande, the antique market in Isle sur la Sorge, the pottery and art exhibitions, the deluxe tablecloth vendors were all earmarked, paged and referenced. Other days had been circled for a trip down to the heavenly village of Cassis or to explore the sandy dunes and flamingo reserves of the Camargue Regional Nature Park. They wanted to experience Provençal life and every minute counted.

The Americans stood out from the crowd in their incredibly smart casual clothes: for the men, Ralph Lauren polo shirts, crease- and soil-resistant chinos, plaited leather belts and navy blue jackets all carefully handpicked by their wives, who stood beside them in their equally studied casual clothing ready for their seven days in the French countryside, where few spoke English and no one accepted American dollars — much to their constant amazement. I often wondered if they ever bothered to unpack, because their holiday was spent at such neck-breaking speed. Was there any latitude for the niceties such as lazing around, sleeping in and relaxing? There were lists of must-do places and activities that spread across several pages: so much effort and organisation had gone into their trip; there would be no time for meandering or daydreaming in tranquil villages. Their stamina and fortitude were awe-inspiring, regardless of age. I have given up explaining to clients that a holiday in Provence is much the same as a gym class: it just does you good to be there; everyone should go at their own pace.

The attitude of the English is quite different. Having spent most of their childhood holidays in France, there are few corners of France where they don't go. The English take their free time very seriously, spending most of it sitting in the sun, glass in hand, book open and eyes shut.

On the whole, the Australians were the most capable type of clients: in one case, perhaps a little too resourceful. To my sheer embarrassment, one client had taken a door off the hinges and driven down to the handyman shop to have a fraction shaved from the bottom to stop it scraping and making annoying noises.

Most, however, started their holiday the moment they spied the bottle of red wine on the kitchen table. Stress and tiredness from their hectic lives were the common threads that linked everyone, regardless of nationality.

By the time I met the Woolleys, I was becoming accustomed to the various quirks and peculiarities of my international clientele. Brian was in his early fifties but looked older: exhausted, tense and very preoccupied, weighed down with the pressures of his work at one of

London's most prestigious banks. His wife Joy was desperate to get their lives on a new track and leave the hustle and bustle of London. They lived among various consulates in a very exclusive part of London. Bomb alerts, explosions and a heavy police presence were part of their everyday life and they were asking themselves if this was really how they wanted to spend their days.

A quick trip to Provence in mid-spring eventually changed their lives. During their holiday they found an abandoned, wild black cat hiding in the hedge at the edge of their holiday home between St Rémy and Avignon, which they named Marie. She was heavily pregnant and very distressed and uncomfortable. Both Brian and Joy were mad cat lovers and understood that it was best to let nature take its course as she prepared for her litter of kittens, whose arrival was imminent. Brian's golfing holiday was fast turning into an animal rescue operation. At the local vet's office, the staff said that they could find homes for the adorable kittens, but Marie would be returned to the wild. All possibilities were investigated, but the regulations for travelling with animals were fairly stringent and meant that Marie could not travel with them back to London as she needed vaccinations and a passport, all of which took time that they did not have. Marie was put into a cattery where she would be well looked after and the Woolleys went back to London to see how they could bring the cat to England.

This was the impetus that they needed to have a complete about-face, leaving behind their drab banker's life in London. They had often toyed with the daydream of leaving London and going to live permanently in Provence. With no children to worry about, the biggest problem was Brian's job and how he was going to be able to walk away from wonderfully remunerated employment. It was not going to be easy to drag Joy out of Harrods and Harvey Nichols, but they wanted to think about downsizing their belongings and making a fresh start. The simple life had great appeal.

Brian found me on the Internet and rang one evening, booking into Rose Cottage for a fortnight's holiday in late spring with a view to looking around the area for a rental property with a large garden that was available from late June to the end of the year. Joy was already booking airline tickets while I was finishing my conversation with Brian.

At the end of their fortnight, they invited me for a drink and a chat. We sat outside Rose Cottage, next to the prolific rose bushes, listening to the water splashing into the little fountain at the end of the square. They didn't have to say very much. I knew what was coming, as every guest said much the same thing: about how they wanted to change their life, move to France, run a guesthouse. In short, looking enviously at me, they wanted my lifestyle. Joy sat transfixed in her chair, aghast: 'Oh no, you have to be kidding! There is no way that we want to run guesthouses or spend hours washing and ironing. No, you misunderstand. I don't want to be rude about your lifestyle choices, but we couldn't think of anything worse to do. And we certainly haven't come here to spend time playing canasta with a bunch of gossips. You see, all I want is a garden where we can sit and play with our cats and basically spend our time doing the crosswords and drinking a glass of rosé. Isn't that right, Brian?'

Brian nodded his head in assent, adding that he quite liked pastis as well; the aniseed-flavoured drink goes so wonderfully with fat black olives or slices of crunchy bread spread copiously with tapenade, the paste made from olives, oil, lashings of garlic and liberal doses of Provençal herbs. He was almost drooling in anticipation as he popped a little slice of baguette into his mouth. We observed Brian savouring his tapenade with such evident relish that he had passed into a state of total oblivion, making little noises of delight as the oily paste slipped over his tongue.

I asked them what they had done during their fortnight stay. They hadn't done much nor gone far but the straining button that was valiantly trying to hold Brian's shorts together and the ample oversized T-shirt that Joy was wearing gave away the fact that they were victims of the Provençal Banquet Belly. They had managed to sample most of the culinary delights available in late spring, several times over.

As the ice cubes melted in their glasses, they, too, drooped and wilted into the furniture. Their eyes had that glassy look and I knew that they were beyond help. They were addicted to Provence.

Did I know of any property that was large, comfortable and had a large garden, appropriate for a couple of docile cats? Bingo. Villa Agapanthe was available. Was it suitable for them? My biggest dilemma was their cats; there were not just two docile cats like ours. Wild Marie from St Rémy was desperate to break out from the cattery and there would be three other black cats from London; their passports and travelling baskets were at the ready.

We scheduled a meeting for the next day to view Villa Agapanthe, which they loved at first sight. It was perfect for their needs, but the biggest stumbling block was the question of heating — or rather, the lack of heating. Having lived in London and all over Europe, they had survived many a brutal winter. They were quite prepared to downsize the dimensions of their new home but certainly not to give up their basic comforts — comforts that I couldn't provide. Another meeting was scheduled with Nathalie the bank manager.

Grasping reams of paper of projected rentals that I had prepared for the two properties in Saignon and the prospective rental of Villa Agapanthe, I set them all in neat piles in front of Nathalie, who sighed heavily, clearly wishing that she had chosen her friends more wisely. My argument was that if I took out a short-term loan from the bank I would be able to install central heating, thereby ensuring I had paying clients for six additional months, which would pay for the heating and show the bank that I was capable of achieving extraordinary winter occupancy rates — and the cash flow would be marginally better. My project of keeping the three holiday homes operational while living in the Wild Thyme Patch was doomed in the long term, but this plan would push the inevitable sale of one or two of the properties back a couple of months. I pushed up my sleeves and asked what the rate was and where I should sign. No, she couldn't put this application through. The bank would not accept my reasons. The party was over for me. No more money from the bank was coming my way. Even if the money was available, she added, how on earth would I be able to have central heating installed before July? My papers flew everywhere as I gathered them up and shoved them into the very smart Italian leather briefcase that Raymond had bought me in an effort to make me behave like a true businesswoman. I stormed out of her office, slamming the door.

The options were very limited. I could go cap in hand to my father and crawl on my knees, begging for help. Or I could sell the car and buy something smaller and more economical, and maybe then I would have enough to pay for the central heating. Both options were untenable, but which one was the lesser of the two evils? The words

choked in my throat as my father answered the telephone
from his sister's house in Scotland. As always, Jack was
canny in his perception of the problem. He might have
been on holiday but he had not left his business acumen
behind. After a good ten minutes of him ranting and
raving while I remained stoically silent, he said that he
would lend me the money for the heating only because it
would increase the value of the house when it came to
selling it the following year. We would have to have a
long talk about the state of my finances next month, on
his arrival in France. I breathed a sigh of relief. One thing
had fallen off my list of things to do.

The weeks were ticking by. My first choice of
plumbers to install the central heating was unavailable
until the beginning of November, as was my second
choice. As I went further and further down my list of
plumbers I realised that I would have to go back to
Didier, who had worked on my two properties in
Saignon. During the period that the renovations were
taking place at Rose Cottage the previous year, I had
had several disputes with Didier as he exercised his
right to male dominance. How could I possibly
entertain the thought that this megalomaniac plumber
would have changed within twelve months? Didier said
that he would be there to start on Friday, and that
within ten days everything would be finished. He had
used similar words when he started work on Rose
Cottage and managed to finish more than six weeks

behind schedule — which I had to concede was more to do with the missing pieces of the staircase than the plumbing. I just had to hope that Didier had not told me another pack of lies.

My heart sank at the thought of his team invading the freshly painted rooms, drilling holes and making a mess. I was sure the floor tiles would crack as they laid out the pipes in the narrow space under the house. My fingers were crossed so tightly that the knuckles went white. I could only hope that this time the budget would stay in check and that the central heating and the repairs to the walls would be finished in time for the Woolleys' arrival from London. When their six-month rental contract was drawn up they had been firm in their demand that any work on the house had to be finished by the time they moved in. It was not an unreasonable request.

I had been a fool in my first dealings with tradesmen in Saignon, thinking that a handshake would suffice; now I demanded a signed quote and firm handshake. It was now in the lap of the gods and, of course, someone of equal stature: Didier the Plumber.

The garden was the next problem: how to transform it instantly and who was going to do the job. I needed some fast-growing Provençal natives that would be able to withstand the heat of the summer and the frosts of the winter, to add to the beginnings of a garden that I had planted the previous month. The local nursery was not interested in giving me advice when they saw my meagre budget. There was no way I could buy the size of plants that my heart desired.

As the plumber and his team worked incessantly on the central heating, I worked outside in the garden, ensnaring the aid of anyone who could be talked into a couple of hours of backbreaking work. In Monsieur Perrard's office, Valérie — who had now replaced her wedding magazines with catalogues for cots and other baby paraphernalia — took time out from her columns of figures to pore over her mother's horticultural books and search out Internet sites, researching trees and shrubs that were hardy enough for the rigours of the Provençal climate.

Amanda continued to work at my files; when no one was looking she would jump on a bike and cycle up to the café in the village to indulge in some harmless flirting and some serious pastis drinking, momentarily escaping the madness that besieged our family.

CHAPTER SIX

Carpe Diem — Seize the Carp?

The creaking wooden gate of the Wild Thyme Patch swung back and forth with the comings and goings of various tradesmen. As nobody had successfully snapped the loop of iron over the opposite side to ensure that it remained firmly fastened, aided by strong gusts of the Mistral it eventually swung off its hinges and lay in a broken heap beside the gateposts: the entrance to our beautiful new home. School had finished, and as Mimi, Harry and Amanda pedalled their bikes through the gap between the gateposts, they screamed in unison, against the howling wind, that it was perhaps best to leave the gate in the wrecked state, as they found that it was a nuisance to have to get off their bikes to open and shut the crooked thing. Raymond lifted his eyes from his Latin Catullus poetry book, slipping his arm around my waist and planting feather-light kisses at the nape of my neck; he said that he would fix it later. I knew his method of distracting me only too well. Here was yet another thing to add to my list of things to do. Nothing was dropping off the list, but more was being added daily.

Summer had begun and lethargy went hand in hand with the rising temperature. Raymond was exhausted from his first term at university after an absence of thirty years. While he was living with us the previous year, he started a Latin course by correspondence through the University of New England in Armidale. This had whetted his appetite so much that he had decided to become a fully fledged full-time university student, travelling back and forth across the bustling harbour by ferry and bus to the sacred halls of Sydney University. His working days in finance had finished unexpectedly early when he was retrenched due to a boardroom plot. Someone wanted his position in the company, and after months of negotiating behind some of the senior partners' backs, a brutal but bloodless coup had taken place. He was now in enforced retirement, with little to no chance of returning to the workforce in his professional field. He was over fifty and apparently over the hill. The network of acquaintances from his working days had shut down completely. He was tired of being an Aussie battler when the only thing he battled through was the traffic. He cut up his credit cards, kissed goodbye his European appliances in his ultra-chic kitchen and rented out his house with its drop-dead view. His life was immediately simplified as he downsized the rest of his possessions, selling or giving them away. At the age of fifty-three, he packed his grey Nike backpack with his books, paper and pens — two travelling tinnies of beer tucked into the side pockets to combat travel sickness — and set out four times per week to mix it with the other university students, who were young enough to be his children. Things had changed since he was last at university; the mood was very serious, with the students being driven by economic necessity to score high marks and exit quickly into the workforce, whereupon they could begin to repay the government their alarmingly high university fees. Gone were the days of spending idle moments smoking marijuana in the Quadrangle, drinking beers or coffees in Manning House, and only occasionally attending lectures in subjects that would lead to degrees that were rarely needed. In those days, jobs were in plentiful supply with or without degrees. For him, it had been Electrical Engineering and a Master of Business Administration, neither of which had served him particularly well.

Raymond had a well-grounded fear that he was not up to the standard of the young pups who had enrolled in his Latin courses at Sydney University. Piles of holiday reading had accompanied him to the other side of the world and needed to be digested by the end of the month. He roamed around the new house in the search for a quiet corner, carting sheets of notes for forthcoming essays and a notepad covered in fluorescent pink or yellow stickers reminding him of things to do, phrases to employ or difficult Latin words to look up. A glaring omission was evident in his hoard. There were no household handy-hint manuals in either French or English. Yet another do-it-yourself trick I would have to learn: how to hang a gate to a post. I added it to the list.

Summer was setting in with a vengeance. In the early morning, the shutters were unhooked and pushed open, allowing the windows to be thrown wide open to let out the stale night air and let the coolness of the morning rush in. By nine o'clock the shutters were latched together again, and the house was plunged into darkness ready to deal with yet another hot day. Towards six or seven o'clock, in the cool of the evening, the shutters would be thrown open again for a short period until they were closed for the final time at bedtime. It was a lot of opening and shutting of heavy squeaking wooden shutters, but it was a system that worked extraordinarily well. The house remained cool and dark while the temperature outside soared towards the forty-degree mark.

The marked contrasts of my two countries, France and Australia, continued to amaze me. Through 200 years of European settlement, Australians tended to

build homes with large open verandas that cut the heat
from the house. Our forefathers had come from
England and Ireland where unrelenting summer heat
had not been a factor in their lives. Had the convicts
come from the south of France, we would have
incorporated the shutter system into our architecture.
The Australian obsession with thick wall-to-wall carpet
would make a Provençal split his sides with laughter;
centuries of experience have taught them that bare tiles
made from stone or earthenware are the necessities of
life. Meanwhile, I was trying to put the various parts of
the cultural jigsaw puzzle together and work out what
Australian ideas could be integrated into the design of
my latest French property without too much expense.
Having spent most of my adult life living in a large city,
my knowledge of alternative lifestyles was extremely
limited but I had a list of questions to ask at the local
handyman store in Apt, even though I could hazard a
guess at the likely responses:

1. *Rainwater tanks — did they exist?*
2. *Solar panels for hot water — did they exist?*
3. *Windmills — could we harness the strong
    Mistral wind to drive a generator for some or all
    of our electrical needs?*
4. *Water diviners — was there someone who could
    assess whether our property was on the all-
    important water table?*

5. *Pyrethrum sprays — were these natural sprays available to deter insects from my roses and from the vegetable garden I wanted to create behind the house?*

I was trying my best to adapt and rise to the numerous challenges of the Wild Thyme Patch. Apart from the continual financial problems, with all of us living under the same roof it was evident that the house lacked space and the convenience of modern appliances such as hot water in the bathroom, cupboards in the bedrooms and heating for winter. A magic wand or a major win in the lottery was needed to create a magnificent home, because my budget had very limited stretch. Nothing was going to happen fast so, like the Provençals, I needed to slow right down, ease back and begin to learn to live the country life. Fast knowledge was best learnt slowly.

The early mornings were undoubtedly the most useful time of the day, before the heat drove the energy from our bodies and thoughts from our minds. Amanda and the children would sleep until midday, having exhausted themselves the previous day with the sun, the public pool in the village and cycling around the neighbourhood. I was so busy and stressed that I never noticed that Amanda's sheer exhaustion was not due to the demands I made on her clerical services during the day, but more to do with her nocturnal wanderings as she sampled the village nightlife. The vast quantities of aspirin that disappeared from the bathroom cabinet should have given me a clue, since I'd been down this party-girl road myself in my younger days. The new English satellite television service that had been installed at great expense was running well into the small hours of the morning, since programs were broadcast one hour later due to the time difference, meaning the nine o'clock program started at ten o'clock in France. At midnight, Amanda and the children would stagger off to their respective beds to arise just before lunchtime the next day.

One morning Raymond and I got up early; opening shutters quietly was my task while his was to make a large pot of tea to take into the garden, where we went to sit in silence. Over our first cup of tea, he began to read some Latin poetry to me, while I stared aimlessly, lost in admiration of the wonderful purplish tinge across the Luberon hills in the distance, growing darker with the progression of the morning. Sometimes the colour of the hills was almost the same as the beautiful mauve silk kimono that I wore to cover my early morning nakedness. In the background was the low but constant chugging and whirling of the washing machine, trying to complete another load of white sheets before seven o'clock, when the electricity went from the night-time cut rate back to the regular daytime rate. We sat together under the large pine tree contemplating the forthcoming day's events, savouring the silence of the moment. Golden moments like these would be not be possible for much longer. More family visitors were due to arrive from various parts of Europe later in the week, and then the house would positively explode with guests — aunts, uncles, grandfather and other extended family members.

I looked up sharply at Raymond: 'If you don't mind, Raymond, go and do that downwind! What on earth have you been eating? That's worse than rotten eggs!'

Raymond leapt up in his own defence, pulling me by my arm, dragging me to the edge of the pond.

'It's the fishpond that smells — not me! Come on. Move it. We have a serious problem.'

Overnight, the beautiful opaque emerald fishpond that stood in front of the house had become a putrid yellowish colour, full of fluorescent lime-green slime. The once clean and uncontaminated water was now tainted; the fetid odours were overpowering. The pond was dying before our eyes. The ponds and the fish swimming in them were really the only things of value on the whole property and they had to be saved.

I had fallen seriously in love with the fish the first time I saw them, when Mimi and I first came to the Wild Thyme Patch. The property had three large ponds. The largest was gigantic, with two small islands in the middle, one of which was reached by a high arching bridge, Japanese in style. The deepest end was over a metre deep, perfect for the pond life but not safe for humans to swim in. Swimming in the pond would never be an option, no matter how high the mercury rose. It was home to a host of aquatic life, ranging from the innocuous large croaking frogs and the pretty transparent blue dragonflies flitting between the lily pads to the odious black water snakes; in short, it was the ideal home for my massive koi carp and their friends, but not for us humans. The second and much smaller pond was close to the house and, having a much smaller volume, the fish in it were not giants. The third pond lay empty in the middle of my higgledy-piggledy orchard of plum, cherry and almond trees, the fallen cherries seeping into the cement floor in large ugly blotches, wide cracks as thick as fingers zigzagging across the cement. The ponds remained because of their beauty but none of them was particularly watertight.

I had already come to love sitting beside the large pond, watching the five magnificent koi carp gliding in the water between the leaves of the immense and prolific water lilies. This was my private little oasis where Zen calm reigned and where no dreaded eels lived. But not this morning. The calm was shattered as I began to scream slightly hysterically, rushing around begging the fish not to die in the rotten brew. Raymond, as always, was composed and unruffled: 'Calm down. Go and get dressed. Wake the children and Amanda. We will need their help immediately. Go find some large buckets. We'll transfer them into the other pond while we work out what to do with this one.'

At that moment, the plumber's white van came through the gate, too fast as usual, grinding to a halt and sliding along the fine white gravel to a complete standstill. Thin plumes of chalky dust rose from the gravel as Didier descended from the van's cabin, cigarette clenched between his yellowish teeth, hand extended.

'*Bonjour, madame. Bonjour* Raymon'.' Didier's every action, every word, made the ire rise in me — even the polite niceties seemed to have a double meaning. Had I not asked him never to come to the house before eight o'clock unless we had a previous arrangement? Just as I had asked him not to drive into the driveway too fast as there were always children around. He had laughed, sniggered even, when I told him what I would do to him and his cigarette if I caught him smoking and throwing away his butts in my garden. He was a slippery eel, with his eyes forming narrow slits, calculating my every move. And I have always had a strong antipathy towards eels. I wished with all my might to kick him hard in the shins. But Didier and his motley crew were installing the central heating in the Villa Agapanthe, just a kilometre or two up the road. His day of reckoning would have to wait.

He walked over to shake hands. The year before, I had been initiated into the correct etiquette of a French building site. Every time I saw one of the tradesmen with their hand extended and a '*bonjour*' rolling off their tongue, I was expected to reciprocate, shaking their forearm if their hands were dirty. I spent a lot of time shaking hands, saying *bonjour* and asking about their health as they tried to hide a burning cigarette in their other hand. Generally we would pass a good fifteen minutes going through the list of social niceties consisting of health, sleeping patterns and the family's wellbeing. Then and only then was it deemed acceptable to start the morning's sparring about the latest catastrophe.

Didier was very sprightly this particular morning, as he wanted to tell me the good news that he expected to finish the complete installation of the central heating within forty-eight hours. I waited for the large 'but' that tradesmen normally attached to the end of their sentences, throwing me further into doom and gloom. Instead he stood there rocking on his heels, extremely pleased with himself.

'*Eh, madame*, you didn't think that I could do it, but I would like you to come at nine o'clock and I will show you our progress.' He wrinkled his nose in disgust as a pungent aroma wafted towards him. He looked at Raymond accusingly until he saw the bubbles rising from the pond. '*Mon Dieu,* what has happened to your pond? *Oh là là!* Your fish, they will die. Do not worry, *madame*, I will help you. You Australians are limited in your knowledge about ponds. I, on the other hand, happen to know what to do. Your favourite plumber is here to save the day.' I was sure by the end of the day I would kick him.

Raymond cannot stand any type of confrontation, so he thought it would be best to leave Didier and me to a discussion that would be sprinkled with expletives. He excused himself to go to the attic to wake the heavily sleeping children. Fish had to be saved. Large pots to transport them had to be found. Nets to scoop them from the pond would make the job faster and safer for the distressed and dying fish. Already my voice was raised and I started to jab the air with my index finger as I itemised priorities.

Didier had come to the same conclusion and encouraged me to leave as soon as possible on a mercy dash to buy large nets at the nearest fishing shop, which was in Cavaillon, thirty-four kilometres away — at least a half hour's drive — saying gently that I should stop flapping my arms around like a demented bird. Although he found my exotic mauve silk kimono particularly alluring, he suggested that it was perhaps not the best attire for the streets of Cavaillon. I stomped off, cross that yet again Didier was correct on too many fronts. Firstly, I had forgotten that we had made an appointment to meet before the start of the working

day at Villa Agapanthe so that we could discuss some
new problems I was having with the agricultural
watering system in the Wild Thyme Patch. Secondly, I
had forgotten that I was still in my kimono. During the
course of the next two days, I found out two things
that made me even crosser with myself and with
Didier:

1. *The sleeves of my beautiful silk kimono did not
    conceal the globes of my bouncing breasts.*
2. *There was a very large fishing shop that sold all
    fishing supplies, including large nets, in Apt — just
    ten kilometres away.*

By the time I was dressed and leaving, Didier had
telephoned his team and they had downed tools at Villa
Agapanthe to come to the fish rescue. They arrived one
after another, skidding across the white gravel. Yet again,
plumes of gravel dust blew up and surrounded them as
they sauntered lazily towards me. The Magnificent Trio
had arrived: Didier's nephew Nicholas, aged twenty-five;
the apprentice, who was another of Didier's nephews,
Nicholas II, aged eighteen; and Nicholas the gardener,
aged twenty-four. There was also Laurent the electrician,
aged thirty, whom nobody particularly liked. Not one of
these men would normally have an adjective like
'magnificent' attached to their name, but that morning I
was so grateful to have three-and-a-half able-bodied

men at my disposal. Laurent could only count as half as he was overweight and already perspiring heavily. He had come on Didier's request to look at my very ancient electrical board and to give me a quote for replacing the system so that it would conform to the latest safety requirements. He slipped inside to look at the board and to get out of doing anything that resembled physical activity. Despite his bulk, Laurent was also very eel-like.

We took fifteen minutes to go through our *bonjour* and handshaking ritual. Everyone had slept well. Tick. Everyone was fine. Tick. No illness. Tick. Children well. Tick. Wife well. Tick. No dirty hands. Tick. Problem at hand: the water in the pond had turned and the fish needed to be removed before they all died. As I said that, the first of the tiny fish popped to the surface, belly up.

Raymond did not speak French so it was pointless leaving him in charge. Didier stepped forward and told me to hurry to Cavaillon for the nets. Luckily, he said, he had ordered the mini-digger for the day. I turned on him: 'What mini-digger? What would you be using a mini-digger for? We have not discussed this.'

'*Madame*, the digger is to dig the trenches that you will want when we discuss the problems with the agricultural water system that you have here on the property. I will need to dig some trenches and lay pipes across the back section. *Ah oui, madame,* it is true that we have not discussed this as our meeting was for eight o'clock this morning, nor have I given you a quote for this work as yet, but you will find that this is your only solution. Didier, your favourite plumber, will save the day once again. I ordered the digger for today so that we can start work immediately. *Madame*, I do not have to tell you that 1 August is just around the corner.' Just as he made that final comment, Raymond reappeared, grasping my elbow and steering me towards the car. It was definitely shin-kicking time. I exploded into a long diatribe querying how the French economy could survive when the whole of France closed down partially for the month of July and competely for the month of August; nothing ever got done; nobody worked longer than thirty-five hours, everyone took two hours at lunchtime, and nobody ever started work before eight o'clock in the morning, regardless of the soaring temperatures. In fact, I continued, I hate the bloody French. I hate every single one of them. Raymond kissed me hard on the mouth and pressed against my body, which was shaking with rage.

'Drive safely. Hurry back as soon as possible. You have people who need you back here in one piece. Think of the fish, not Didier. *Mon capitain*, their little lives depend on you.' He stood to attention with his hand in a salute as I drove off towards Cavaillon. It enraged me that he could be so offhand about this dire situation. Raymond waltzed back and forth into our lives as he saw fit. Since he had left the year before I had been completely alone and in charge and it was important to me that I assumed complete responsibility for my financial and emotional life. I had a vague plan for the financial side but the emotional side would have to wait.

The moment I was out of sight, the pecking order was assumed. Didier would take charge because he was a real man — he did not sit around with Latin poetry books sipping tea in the garden. Secondly and perhaps most importantly, he had a great depth of knowledge about how to deal with all problems arising from plumbing, life and that necessary evil — women.

The children and Amanda came tumbling down the stairs from the attic, only to be dispatched back up them again to search for some large zinc tubs that Didier had seen the day he had been in the attic looking for a mysterious leak in the roof. Meanwhile, Raymond looked for something larger than a tea strainer to scoop up the smaller fish. The one and only net that we had was in the safe hands of Nicholas II, who was galloping around the pond on his imaginary white charger, brandishing his net in front of him like a lance, doing his best to bring his bulging biceps into sharp relief under his tight white cotton T-shirt.

On my return, the scene had become even more chaotic, with Didier thigh deep in the pond, catching fish with his bare hands. Nicholas II was trying to emulate his uncle but to no avail. The children were rushing back and forth between the ponds, splashing most of the water from the pots as they delivered the distressed fish into the smaller pond. Mimi was scooping up the fish that had jumped or been sloshed out of the buckets onto the ground. The young men had stripped down to their jeans, exposing their divine young torsos — lean, muscular and heavily tanned. They looked like Greek gods at play. Then I saw the reason why: Amanda. The young men's eyes were on swivel sticks as they watched her every move. They flexed their muscles as they carried the large zinc hipbaths back and forth to the small pond. They preened and posed. Their inadvertent comic relief made the situation slightly more bearable.

Didier had made the executive decision in my absence to drain the pond of all the muck and putrefying plant life. Nicholas was seated in the mini-digger brandishing the trowel, scooping up the detritus from the pond. Sandals and shoes were lined up along the edge of the main pond as everyone was sliding around, the mud oozing between their toes as they attempted to catch as many fish as possible in the small amount of stinking water that was left. There were cries of joy and exasperation as they scooped up the mud and the fish with the large nets. Even Laurent had come to lend a hand and had installed himself under the pine tree in a comfortable chair, delicately sifting through the mud for fish. Didier called out in high excitement that finally he had one of the largest fish.

'*Madame*, go and fetch the bathroom scales. Let's see how much this fish weighs!'

I had never realised that the fish were quite as big as this. They were enormous. Didier jumped on the scales without the fish and then with the fish: 7.4 kilos. Laurent looked up lazily and asked if they were good eating fish.

The oppressive heat was now almost unbearable and some of the smaller fish were dying from shock and the rapid change in habitat. The pond floor was hosed out and most of the remaining mud shovelled out. It was time to fill up the pond as quickly as possibly.

'Didier, which is the tap for the agricultural water to fill up the pond? Isn't it lucky that we have that? It would cost a small fortune to use the drinking town water. This pond is so big it would take more water than a normal size swimming pool.'

'*Eh oui, madame* — as usual you are right. But that was something that I wanted to talk to you about this morning. You have in fact the cheap water supply connected to this property but you must go to Cadenet this week and pay for a reconnection fee. If you do not do this before 1 August there is no way that you will have it during the heat of summer and even then maybe not before the middle of September.' Raymond understood enough French to get the gist of Didier's words. He stepped in front of Didier as I gave myself over to my mounting rage. I would have to pay for full price drinking water for the Luberon's most expensive fish.

Later that week, I stopped off at the aquaculture showroom on the road to Avignon where they sold all types of water fountains, water lilies, real and fake rocks, thick black plastic liners for do-it-yourself ponds, plastic floating birds and other exotic creatures to place around the garden and pond. I spoke to Monsieur de Moncuit and begged him to make a home visit. I needed his advice to ensure the security of my fish and the vastly diminished pond life.

Two days later he arrived to inspect my pond. It was like a school inspection. I waited anxiously for my report card. As he took samples of the water I could see that I was failing miserably. He pulled on some thick waders and went to the middle of the pond to retrieve the floating remnants of the lilies and begin his silent work repotting them into specifically designed aquatic pots with perforated holes.

'*Madame*, this pond is in terrible state. The plants must be grouped together so that the fish can have as much shade as possible. You must leave that hose running day and night until I get you a suitable pump that will recycle this water, giving the fish the oxygen that they need desperately. If only you had rung me before you emptied the pond. Never, ever empty a pond, *madame*. It has taken years to build up a fine ecosystem that was perfect for those fish. All that was necessary was to put the hose into the pond for forty-eight hours and the problem would have righted itself, saving you the disaster that you yourself created.'

There was no way that I would understand country life, I was just too much of a city slicker. There was a good chance that the pond life would survive, but I wasn't sure that I would survive his account, which he handed to me saying that there was a small discount given if paid within fourteen days.

CHAPTER SEVEN

Domus Latina

With the increasing heat of summer, one day melted into another as we got used to the routine of the new house and having two additions to the family: Raymond and Amanda. Subconsciously or consciously I was looking for more ways to bring Raymond back into our life on a permanent basis, and it was obvious that it would take more than English television to make him want to stay. I couldn't understand why he didn't feel the same way as I did about living in France or why he didn't want to live with the children and me. He loved us, of that I was sure, but as he said time after time, how can you want to live in a country where the language is so strange? He would cite his favourites: vagina — *le vagin* was a masculine word; cock — *la bite* was feminine. It was pointless to counter-cite the beauty of the language and the culture. Unfortunately my habit of making lists had rubbed off on him, so periodically he would rearrange his Top Ten French Faults depending on what latest news item had provoked his ire:

1. *They were linguistically insane.*
2. *They were doomed to economic failure with the pursuit of the thirty-five hour week.*
3. *They refused to initiate microeconomic reforms.*
4. *They refused to acknowledge the growing social problems that existed in France and were becoming more evident with the lack of education and growing unemployment in the Arab community.*
5. *Ethnic urban ghettos were allowed to grow unchecked due to archaic political strategies.*
6. *Television programs did not start on the hour or half hour.*
7. *'1664' was inadequate as a beer.*
8. *There were more than 365 cheeses in France and yet none of them was remotely like good English cheddar.*
9. *Strolls in the French countryside were off limits during hunting season due to the numbers of accidental shootings that occurred.*
10. *Quality, age and provenance were considered the most important factors in red wine, as opposed to quantity, a prized Australian attribute.*

Our first try at long-term domesticity had come a little unstuck the previous year, when I had spent a great deal of time screaming at everyone as the tension over house renovations in Saignon hit fever pitch. Life was definitely calmer nowadays. We had turned a corner. The renovations were complete, and although my small business was struggling through a very grim period, I was confident that I would avoid bankruptcy and the forced sale of the properties. At three o'clock one morning, I hit upon an idea. It was becoming increasingly obvious to me that deep in my heart I did not want to — and was not able to — make a clean break from Raymond. If he hadn't irritated me so much, and if we'd both lived on the same continent, maybe I could have fallen hopelessly, completely and utterly in love with him — yet again. It was the same old question that had occupied my mind ever since Norman died: would my children benefit from having a substitute father figure? How much happiness did Raymond bring into my life that then flowed into my children's lives? Did he bring stability into my life, making me a better mother? Was I kidding myself about my love for Raymond? Did I in fact just need another adult to help raise my children? I couldn't bring myself to admit defeat over our floundering relationship. The only solution was to make him fall so madly in love with me that he would not leave — and that would not happen unless he had his own private space. Then I could dispatch him back to Australia when it suited me.

In Australia, there was an unwritten agreement between spouses that the 'bloke' — the husband or the eldest male of the tribe — could claim the garden shed in the backyard, where he could slip away for a few solitary moments each week to read the sports section of the Saturday paper while listening to the cricket or the rugby on a little transistor radio, affectionately called his 'trannie', while he drank a couple of beers called 'tinnies'. Nowadays 'trannie' means transvestite, and in the world of iPods and MP3s nobody even knows what a transistor looks like any more. There were some accepted rules in Australian society, one of which was: women are not allowed to approach The Shed — it was for men's business only. The female elders could discuss their Secret Women's Business with the girls on card nights, at bowls or on the golf course or tennis court, and the younger women could do the same while waiting for children at the school gate, helping out at the school canteen, watching children's sport or sitting through interminable music or ballet lessons or private tutoring. It was an unwritten Australian law that men and women needed their own space. I set out to investigate every room and every shed on the property for its potential as a Latin Study.

The previous German owners were passionate gardeners and had large compost pits dotted all over the property for grass clippings, vegetable matter and old horse manure, and there were numerous sheds to house all of the equipment needed to keep the land looking its very best. At the back of the property was a large run-down second garage that was in a fair state of repair. There was even a lean-to where a small car or a trailer could be parked under shelter. There was ample room to put the lawnmower, rakes, shovels, spades, axes and picks and just about every other gardening implement the previous owners appeared to own in triplicate and the many different sizes and kinds of jerry cans and oils they'd had to keep everything in impeccable Germanic running order. When I first saw the property, I couldn't help noticing that the wooden handle on each implement had been sanded back and linseed oil applied to stop the wood cracking. They were lined up in neat vertical lines, attached by hooks to the back wall. The blades of the shovels had been cleaned and washed of mud, sharpened with a whetstone, oiled, and then placed into buckets of sand to avoid contact with the hard cement floor that would dull the blades. You could see that there was a great sense of devotion to the garden. Originally, I had aimed to keep my meagre gardening equipment in the same shed, though perhaps not in such a pristine way. But the windows had no glass panes and some roots from nearby trees were making an appearance through the cement floor, which had cracked with age and neglect. The garage was not particularly weatherproof, so it was no good for my new project.

In the run-down orchard there were the remnants of a very large deluxe chicken coop. The original French owners who had built the house in 1965 had obviously designed it with the idea of having extra space for relatives to stay overnight. The roof was sound. The guttering was still in place. Unfortunately there was a major problem with the walls: fissures ran from the ceiling to the floor, where there were large gaps down to the exposed foundations. I am not sure whether any relative ever stayed there, but it was a poultry palace fit for the fussiest chickens. It was a large rectangular construction, almost twenty metres by five metres, with two smallish rooms and one enormous room featuring perches zigzagging along its full length and nesting holes at one end. The rampant weeds from the orchard had found their way into the coop and were rife. Jean-Louis Chiffot, a builder who came to do some minor repairs during our first week in the new house, gave me some free advice: tear it down. It was not habitable; it was starting to look dangerous with its tilt to one side. I had fleetingly entertained the thought that in the autumn I would buy some chickens, thus giving us daily free-range eggs. However, nobody in our household particularly liked eggs, and I was sure that there was no way I could chop off a chicken's head with an axe — even though we could then eat hormone-free free-range corn-fed chicken. Another building was struck from my Latin Study list. This left the upstairs area of the main house or the large freestanding shed near the driveway.

This wonderful shed next to the house was just back from the gaping hole where the brown wooden gates had been. When I bought the property, it had been described in the paperwork as a ten metre by five metre potting shed. It was here that the couple had spent hours — or maybe it was just the husband, as the day I made my first inspection of the property he had been potting up bulbs from large carefully labelled vats into earthenware tubs of all sizes and shapes. Bags of every type of soil had been stacked up high on the shelves. There were poisons, insecticides and sprays. Along one of the walls was a large board a bit like a child's puzzle: so that every tool could go back into its correct position, the tool's outline had been painted black in sharp contrast against the white board. It was homemade and looked very impressive. There were endless open boxes of nails, hooks and screws. It was a dream space for the home handyman. This would be the ideal place for Raymond to have as his private male space. His own garden shed. His own Latin House — a 'Domus Latina'.

I reasoned that I could sacrifice certain of my needs in order to give Raymond his Domus Latina, and then he would stay with me in our sunny part of France and love my children and me. It was asking quite a bit from a humble garden shed, but I prided myself on my creative thinking.

Under the grime I saw on my first visit, there was a smooth cement floor that although not tiled, was more than adequate if it could be cleaned and polished. Now, on further investigation, I could see that the building was solidly built, with excellent floors and wide windows. Not that I knew very much about roofs, but it appeared to be solid, with no dips or missing tiles. In the Luberon, many garden sheds of this type turn magically into rental accommodation of some sort as soon as the building inspector has left, becoming very exotic and expensive *cabanons* — rustic cabins or country cottages — for the unsuspecting foreign tourists looking for an authentic experience in Provence. This shed would be perfect for my plan. I was sure that if I gave Raymond the Latin House, he would stay with me forever. That was exactly what I wanted at three o'clock in the morning, a time when I always seem to be awake solving my latest dilemma.

~

In the midst of our drama concerning the fishponds I had seen yet another job that needed to be added to the list to make life a little better in our new house. All the wood on the little Japanese-styled bridge needed replacing, as it was looking very wobbly and unsafe. The tile capping around the pond edge needed replacing or re-cementing into place, as there were places where it had fallen off into the pond. Now that there was a small quiet pump circulating the water day and night, giving the fish the oxygen that they required, it was time to see how we could reasonably improve the overall look of the pond. I started jotting down a list of things in descending order of priority; this time the pond would definitely come last:

1. *Install lines to hang out the washing.*
2. *Remove the wall in the shed to make one open space.*
3. *Waterproof the third pond as a holding pond while repairs were carried out on the main fishpond.*
4. *Replace all the rotten planks on the bridge over the main pond.*
5. *Replace or repair all the tiles around the main pond.*

'Dig a hole for a pool,' cried out Amanda. She had not spent enough time with me to know that was the last thing to mention. Everyone glared at Amanda. I did feel just a little sorry for her that her summer was mostly being spent indoors surrounded by my files, computer and paperwork.

The team of Ahmeds who had previously worked for me on the renovations to Rose Cottage were called in to do the work at our new house. A smiling black-bearded

Ahmed arrived, flashing his very white teeth. In tow was his equally swarthy cousin Ahmed, to help install the washing lines. By lunchtime the next day, as soon as the cement had set, I would be able to try them out — sixty metres of line in the Provençal sunshine would soon be at my constant disposal. One problem had fallen off the list, only to be replaced by another even more pressing problem: the little four-kilo washing machine would not go the distance. Raymond's Domus Latina was shunted further down the list as I had to rethink how I was going to accomplish the enormous task of weekly washing.

Once, while bent over yet another basket of white sheets, the tears began rolling down my cheeks as I added up the amount of washing I had to do each week. Three beds in Rose Cottage, four beds in Place de la Fontaine, four beds in Villa Agapanthe and four beds in our home — that brought it to a grand total of fifteen beds and hours of work. Every Saturday there were twenty-one people in fifteen beds in four houses, which meant:

Fifteen doona covers
Fifteen bolster covers — *traversins*
Forty-two pillowcases (two pillows per person)
Fifteen mattress protectors
Five tablecloths
Twenty-one cloth serviettes
Twelve tea towels

Sixteen fluffy dressing gowns
Sixteen white extra large towels (clients only)
Twenty-one coloured towels
Twenty-one hand towels
Twenty-one washing mitts

And that wasn't even counting our clothes. I started to howl when I realised that I had not counted the linen used by our summer guests.

In Apt there were two public laundromats, both owned by a man named Roger. I was one of his best customers, spending the best part of Sunday in one or both of his laundromats, rushing from one end of town to the other to pull the sheets from the super large fifteen kilo washing machines into the massive twenty-five kilo tumble drier. It cost a fortune, but a good deal less than having the laundry professionally washed and ironed. Tempers frayed when the machines ate the coins or worse still, not enough coins could be found. When Roger said that he had two second-hand top-of-the-range Miele machines available for sale, I jumped at the chance and blurted out that I wanted them. If I could afford to pay for them, the next question would be: where would I put them?

At the lines the next day, over the passing of pegs and straightening out of sheets, all of my problems fell rapidly into order, and suddenly my priorities were clear. It was an epiphany of sorts.

In Sydney, I had not wanted Raymond to live full-time with us after Norman had died. We had never planned a life of togetherness. I did not want to be bound hand and foot to a man ever again. Deep down in the core of my heart I knew that something was lost when Norman died — the recipe for that wonderful glue that sticks relationships together and seals marriages with monogamy and commitment — together forever. During our early years of marriage we were in the process of concocting it together, but I think Norman took it with him when he passed away. For the best part of my adult life, I had waited for some male to arrive on a white charger ready to whisk me onto the back of his horse; we would gallop away into the sunset where problems did not exist. During the two years here in France, I had come to the conclusion that in fact I did not need nor want a man to rescue me. They were my hands holding the reins of the white charger. I had rescued myself.

Raymond would have to ponder these questions about life for himself, but at the age of fifty-three I thought that it would be highly unlikely that he would suddenly want to change into a second-in-command, always playing second fiddle to me. Raymond was planning to spend a sum total of eight weeks per year in France with us. It did not make any sense to dedicate a building to him just on the off-chance that he would change his mind, enrol in an university in England and spend all of his half-terms and holidays with us in Provence. What on earth was I thinking?

No. I would not give him the Latin House, his Domus Latina — instead I would give it to me as a proper industrial laundry with large efficient machines that would make my life easier. The decision was made. Domus Latina would stay mine. I would turn it into a workshop, specialising in ironing and washing. I would stop having girlish fantasies about knights in shining armour or true love. I would get back to basics:

1. *Keep the children happy.*
2. *Keep the house — especially the oven — sparkling clean.*
3. *Keep the sheets white and freshly ironed.*
4. *Break up with Raymond and get on with my life.*

Didier, my favourite plumber, came to give me a quote for the additional plumbing that would be required. I was feeling a lot friendlier towards him after his extremely rapid job on the central heating that turned out to cost less than the original quote. Now he explained that we would need to bring the agricultural water from one end of the property to the other; he gave me explicit reasons why I should have seemingly thousands of kilometres of extra trenches dug all across the land. The new pipes would service the ponds and the area that was earmarked for the magnificent swimming pool — 'where was the money coming for that?' I bleated. He rapidly drew red and blue zigzags and loops across the back of a piece of paper, sketching a rough diagram of where the main house, garden sheds, ponds and garages stood. A red line showed where X marked the spot — the newly christened *atelier*, or workshop. The huge industrial washing machine would be serviced by agricultural water. This water was for watering crops, so it cost less than ten per cent of the normal price of drinking water. It was not crystal clean, but if Didier installed a filtration system, with salination pumps to soften the water and larger pipes to take the pressure from the industrial pipes, I could wash the whole of the Luberon's laundry for a fraction of the normal cost. The downside was that his nephew Nicholas would need to dig up the whole of the garden to install pipes, as per the tatty red and blue diagram that he brandished under my eyes. He would have to dig around in circles and back again and then some more loops across the driveway, break many existing pipes, fix the leaking pond and then leave me in a hellish mess just in time for the whole of France to begin their month-long holiday, starting on the dreaded 1 August. It sounded a perfect idea.

So it was decided. Didier's team of Nicholas nephews was coming back and along with them the great slug, Laurent the electrician. On the day of the Great Fish

Drama, Laurent had a good look at my electrical situation and pointed out that if I was installing a large industrial washing machine and a dryer in the workroom, new wiring and a new board would be needed as there was no way the present archaic equipment would cope with the large machines for more than one minute. Due to my determination to show Raymond that I was now an independent and astute businesswoman, I shook hands with everyone and agreed to their hideous terms. No man was going to have a say in the running of my business, except perhaps my father, and there was no way that I was going to tell *him* that I had bought a house without sufficient bedrooms, cupboards, storage space and heating and with a woefully inadequate electrical board.

I still hadn't adequately learnt that fundamental lesson: never undertake any sort of building or repairs unless there is a written quote, preferably written in the boss's blood; a verbal contract is not worth spit. And spitting I was when I realised the foolhardy adventure I had embarked on. The plumbers had asked the electricians, who had asked the gardener to the party, and I found out later that I was paying for a huge amount of work that was vaguely justified but perhaps would have been better left till a lot later in the year.

Once the decision had been made to create a workshop, Roger was contacted immediately to see when he could deliver the fifteen-kilo washing machine and the twenty-five kilo tumble dryer. In my ignorance, I assumed that the machines could be delivered and plugged into the wall like any other machine — at the most, three-phase wiring might be needed. My sister Kate had had an electric kiln when she was a mad-keen potter as a teenager, well before children and life ate into her time, and I remembered that an electrician had installed three-phase wiring for the big silver monster. Did it depend on the size of the machine? I hesitated to ask my least favourite electrician, Laurent, about this problem.

Raymond had watched from the sidelines as I rushed about asking for information about the property's wiring but he could no longer sit idle, as he had made a list of problems that needed to be fixed:

1. *The house needed new wiring.*
2. *Safety switches were needed on a second electrical board set up in the workshop.*
3. *A massive gas reservoir was needed to run the machines.*
4. *A concrete slab was needed to support the gas reservoir.*
5. *Another concrete slab was needed to support the machines in the workshop.*

6. *A water supply was needed, either expensive town water or the cheap agriculture supply (Raymond held his breath over that issue).*

7. *I needed to pay for this latest venture — and how would I do that when I already reeled back in horror every month with the mortgage repayments? (Raymond was now red in the face, stabbing his finger in the air.)*

8. *We were not to break up now because I needed him and more than anything, he loved me.*

9. *It was all out of the question.*

～～

It was time to make an appointment to see Nathalie, my bank manager. When I bought the Wild Thyme Patch I managed to secure a loan for twenty years at 3.35 per cent — an outstanding deal. Now I was looking at a short-term loan for ten years and the best rate was 5.20 per cent — certainly not brilliant, but having the *atelier* would make running the properties easier. It was not possible to employ any help; again the load would fall on my shoulders — a concern voiced loudly by Nathalie. Her fingers flew across the keypad yet again, tallying up my different thinning streams of income. She would put my request through to head office, even though she seriously doubted whether they would be offering me any deals. It was the best that she could do. I began to contemplate what I could sell to raise the money in case it didn't come through — how much would I get per child?

Although Didier drove me mad, I had to admit that he and the Nicholases were behaving faultlessly. They were working flat out to a schedule and nothing was going to stop them getting to the end of the agreed work on time — the last day of July. The crippling heat was relentless. No matter how many times our eyes turned skywards in the desperate search for anything that resembled a cumulonimbus formation, the sapphire blue sky remained clear, free from the inky clouds heavy with summer rain needed to break the cycle. It was predicted that the endless monotony of perfect days would continue to stretch well into August. Nature was already on holiday, with very little movement apart from the ants with their busy daily activity. The neighbour's dogs, which barked at the rare passing pedestrian, could barely be bothered to raise their heads; panting heavily, they dozed peacefully in the scant shade offered by the scrappy vegetation in their garden. There was little or no activity in the pond, causing me to check that the fish were still there and had not been spirited away during the night: no movement from frogs, dragonflies or fish. They had taken refuge under the large lily pads spread across the vast expanse of opaque water. Only the slow movements of Didier and the young men interrupted the catatonic scene, as they moved around languidly to conserve their energy. Their mouths parted to inhale deeply on the cigarettes permanently hanging from their mouths, or to take long draughts from the bottles of water that they carted around by the neck. There was no idle chatter. All of their energy was focused on reaching the finish line. It was imperative to complete the task with every problem resolved, otherwise my hand was not going near a chequebook. My fingers were tightly crossed that Nathalie and her bank would come through with the loan before the crucial date of 1 August.

Didier had called in a huge favour from a friend in Avignon who could work a miracle. Slowly but surely I was learning about the system of favours here in Provence: it was imperative to have a large bank of favours at your disposal. The miracle was that it would be possible to have the largest size gas reservoir delivered within forty-eight hours. Given that it normally took a week to ten days, this was phenomenal news. He broke the news to me much later that I would have to wait almost a fortnight for the reservoir to be filled with gas. As a stopgap, large portable gas tanks were rigged up for the kitchen and the hot water.

The forty-eight hours before delivery gave the team of Ahmeds just enough time to check the recently poured concrete slab to see if it had dried and cured. Unfortunately they had never asked me where I wanted the concrete slab for the reservoir. Instead they had made an executive decision, putting it near the workshop and close to the side road for easy gas delivery — which was good — but in the middle of my so-called organic vegetable patch in the making — which was not good. Why hadn't they put it along the side of the fence where it would have been discreetly out of the way?

The day arrived when Didier called me over to the workshop. His youngest nephew Nicholas was playing an imaginary trumpet, heralding the announcement of the great event: the completion of the workshop. Did I want Raymond to carry me over the threshold? Raymond had managed to drag himself out into the midday inferno from the cool dark house and stood there flexing his muscles idiotically. By this stage, the draining heat had beaten my normally ebullient spirit and I was thoroughly fed up with all males and in particular Didier, with his handy words of wisdom on life and on women. I had tempted fate and had unwisely given up feeding the small washing machine its regular stream of soiled linen, convinced that within a few days my problems would be solved as with a flick of the switch, the Miele washing machine would accomplish miracles. Didier, was beside himself with glee that the beautiful machines were ready to operate — and that similar to another all-powerful being, he alone had created this vision, and in only slightly more than seven days. His arms swept through the air as he leapt from one foot to another. The tension was unbearable. It would either work or not. I had placed a huge amount of faith in Roger that these second-hand machines actually worked. Late in July it had been impossible to find a technician who was available to inspect the machines. I had bought them on Roger's good word. I just hoped that it was going to be good enough. I wished that I had some sort of guarantee as a backup.

The sheets were bundled into the machine, the tablets of washing powder thrown into the drum, the switch turned, and we stood back as the machine filled up, gurgling and sucking in the water from the new pipes. Raymond held me in his arms as we looked at the glass porthole of the machine. My new fifteen-kilo, shining stainless steel baby. It was a dream come true. 'Didier, well done!' we cried out with delight. We whooped and screamed with joy — until I saw the filthy brown water. My wonderful white sheets were being washed in water the colour of my morning's café au lait. I looked at Didier.

'Is agricultural water always so dirty and brown? You said that it was clean enough for swimming pools. I wouldn't want to swim in this stuff, let alone wash my linen. Your problem, Didier. You find the solution and find it soon: 1 August is around the corner. You cannot go on holidays until this problem is solved and I certainly will not be paying for it. I hope that's clear.'

Didier's proud puffed-up chest had deflated markedly. It was not quite the success that he had hoped for.

'*Madame,* this is good news, *n'est-ce pas?* Personally, I never thought that the washing machine would work. It has been disconnected for far too long. Machines do not like that. You are very lucky that it works. You have a guardian angel and you have Didier. Do not fear, *madame,* this is only a small problem with the water. My nephews will fix this. There is nothing to worry about at all.'

The sheets were turning the colour of pale chocolate, and even when we returned for the final rinse, hoping against hope that the water would suddenly turn clear and the sheets would rinse clean, the machine was still full of liquid chocolate. Didier shrugged his shoulders and looked for his telephone to call his older nephew Nicholas to bring back the mini-digger. Another trench was needed immediately to bring in the clean town water that had to be connected to the washing machines. The cheap agricultural water would never work.

By this stage, Raymond knew well enough never to laugh at my misfortunes but to try to find the positive in the situation. He whipped the light coffee-coloured sheets away to the newly installed clotheslines to dry under the scorching midday sun, saying that he always wanted sheets just that shade of sepia. I retreated to the kitchen to prepare the midday meal and to smash some pots around in the peace of my domain.

By lunchtime two days later, Didier had the situation completely under control. The trench had been dug. The new pipes had been laid and connected. All systems were go; the next test with clean town water was ready. I looked around the workshop and felt that with all the new equipment, this time success was guaranteed. In the past week, more than the bare necessities had been installed:

1. *A fifteen kilo washing machine.*
2. *A twenty-five kilo tumble dryer.*
3. *A water heater.*
4. *A water softener.*
5. *A 2000 litre gas tank and concrete slab.*
6. *A boiler for the central heating.*
7. *An industrial iron and extra wide ironing board.*
8. *A water filter.*
9. *A chest of drawers to house the washing mitts, hand towels, tea towels and oven mitts.*
10. *A new system of pipes to carry the clean town water to the workshop.*

The heavens smiled. The washing machine worked. Soiled white sheets went in, clean white sheets came out.

Never in my wildest dreams had I thought my life would revolve around a laundry. Now I was in possession of the biggest and undoubtedly the best private laundry in the Luberon.

CHAPTER EIGHT

The House Fairy

I now had a clean, functioning workroom, just slightly too large for my needs but perfectly organised now that all the shelving had been assembled. Piles of white sheets, pillow cases, duvet covers, bolster covers and mattress protectors were sitting in straight rows, each on their correct shelf according to the size of bed — queen, double or king single — all waiting for their next outing on Saturday: Client Changeover Day. It seemed that every week even more linen was required to supply our ever-increasing needs, as the floodgates had been opened, and more family and friends had decided to descend on us.

I had listened to stories from others about the visitors who plagued them almost weekly, and hoped that the same would not happen to us. However, the day the mercury soared upwards the telephone began to ring nonstop — long-lost friends who just happened to be in the area and didn't mind popping in for a couple of days. It was obvious that I had to introduce the Three Day Rule. Family and fish go off after three days.

Claire had offered to unpack and arrange the workshop with me. She was as bossy as ever and never kept still for one moment, but the workshop was transformed with seemingly little effort into a clean and highly organised workspace. She was highly trained and efficient in these matters — which was just as well, as packing and unpacking remains my Achilles heel. A year after our move to France, some boxes still sat in piles at the back of the garage, untouched and unopened after their long voyage from Sydney. My former life was tied up in thick brown paper, packing tape and string. My memories were bound and bundled high in packing crates. I had no desire to revisit them. A small photo of a happy bride and groom lies in my sock drawer. On most days that is comfort enough.

While I was busy manoeuvring Claire, she in turn was doing likewise to me. The large space in front of the machines and the rows of linen shelves was virtually empty, even with the extra large ironing board permanently set up. The large French doors that faced due south gave a beautiful view of the vines and the violet mountains in the background and allowed the sunlight to flood in. An ideal sewing space, she said under her breath.

The upholstery that she had done for Villa Agapanthe had been meticulous. She had arrived with notepad and pen in one hand, tape measure in the other, and went through with me, room by room, working out what needed to be made to give the property that extra bit of polish and style that I was seeking. Curtains, covers for bed bases, tablecloths and slipcovers for chairs were churned from her sewing machine in record time. Everything was a perfect fit and helped make the house exactly the way I needed it to be: comfortable yet very practical. She needed the space that I had in the workroom. Although I thought that it was I who decided everything, I had a fair suspicion that Claire's hand was guiding me gently into place.

'Claire, I have an excellent idea. Why don't you work here in this space? You could put all your bobbins, threads, zips and other haberdashery along this wall and there would be more than enough space for both of your sewing machines. You can have your own key to the workshop. Come and go as you please. What do you think?'

'Yes, in fact, this is a wonderful idea. I'll just go and get my boxes out of the car.' I had the feeling that Claire would always have the upper hand.

We came to an agreement that in return for the sewing area, Claire would come and help me on Saturdays with cleaning and bed making. It didn't take her long to see that I should be confined solely to the basics: bed making, changing light bulbs, rearranging the books and videos and checking the dishwashing and washing powders. My House Fairy would take care of the cleaning and dusting. So Claire moved into my life and trod carefully until she had woven her magic around me, teaching me a few new skills every day. Suddenly I seemed to have twice as many hands:

1. *I had to put a load of washing on — tick. She had done it.*
2. *The washing machine filter had to be checked once a week — tick. She had checked it.*
3. *The linen had to be folded from the tumble dryer — tick. She had folded everything.*
4. *The twenty-kilo bag of salt for the water softener was needed — tick. She had bought it.*
5. *The massive amount of washing powder required had been bought at a discount — tick. And installed in boxes on the shelves.*
6. *The small tears in the sheets needing a stitch — tick. She had done it.*
7. *The floors needed to be constantly swept and washed — tick. All done.*

In fact I was starting to feel quite redundant, but we were both happy helping each other out, and best of all, she just never seemed to be around. The House Fairy seemed to have everything under control, which was handy, since hordes of family and friends were arriving soon.

Meanwhile, Amanda had worked similar wonders with the office: coloured files and folders were set up in bookshelves, neatly labelled with a foolproof coding system of letters and numbers. It was just as well that the office was now in order because with so many houseguests and unannounced visitors at meal times, she was needed as my spare set of hands in the kitchen. Glass in hand, Amanda was chopping and dicing almost full-time in the small kitchen that did not realistically have room for more than two cooks at any one time.

She made salads from carrots, cucumbers, chickpeas, lentils, lettuce or anything else that came her way, letting her imagination run wild. When in doubt, she sat down on the back step gleaning inspiration from the latest sensational Australian cookbooks. I, on the other hand, stayed with things that I had cooked all of my life and seen my mother Sheilagh cook a thousand times over. My favourite was ratatouille, a thick Provençal vegetable stew with zucchini, red, yellow and green peppers, thick slices of eggplant, olives, tomatoes, onions and Provençal herbs, and liberal lugs of olive oil. Since moving to Provence I realised that olive oil was akin to holy water and it had to be treated with respect and referred to only in hushed and revered tones. Vegetables, too, were a revelation: at the market, baskets swinging, we learnt to find whose vegetables were the freshest and the best. The choice was breathtaking. I looked forward to the day when I would be able to grow my own vegetables in the garden surrounding my very large gas reservoir.

On either side of the Wild Thyme Patch stood large fallow fields; in both were crumbling *cabanons* — traditional small cottages — which after decades of neglect were gradually falling into heaps of unloved rubble. In Sydney, our family home was squashed into a row of similar houses, side by side. Here in the Luberon our nearest neighbours, the Two Ladies, lived more than 200 metres away in a modest little house with a wonderful garden. You could tell that it had been tended with a great deal of love and devotion. By the back fence was a tiny patch of tomatoes and other vegetables, trained carefully on wicker sticks set in a tepee shape. In the early evenings I would watch the Two Ladies walk along our unsealed road, taking their two silky terriers and one very fat cat for a walk. Catherine, cigarette hanging precariously from her lower lip, had offered advice when the gates had fallen off their hinges and in a roundabout manner said that at a later date she and her partner Geneviève could start up a vegetable patch for me. As often happens in my life, I liked the concept of a wonderful organic vegetable patch better than the reality of dirty nails, a very sore back at the end of the day and a bad dose of sunburn on the neck and arms. I wanted to show Mimi and Harry that growing our own fruit and vegetables would be cost-effective and very rewarding. I dismissed their snide remarks about worms in the salad and the difficulties of growing pineapples, kiwi fruit and mangoes in the Luberon. I was more than grateful to accept Catherine and Geneviève's offer. Social mores can be difficult to interpret in your own culture, let alone in the French countryside. I wasn't sure whether I was the brunt of a joke or if it was a real offer to be taken up in the not too distant future. I hoped that they had meant it and that one day they would arrive with their boots and shovels.

The August heat was in full force and we eyed houses with pools with envy. The public pool in our village was fabulous for a social gathering but abysmal for any long-distance swimming. My father Jack became the instant star of the pool, diving in one end and coming out the other without his swimming costume. I did not want to go in and show my milky white Celtic skin to anyone, let alone have mothers at the school gate come up and give me handy hints about why French women are never fat. Watching them ash their cigarettes over their own children's hair, I thought wistfully of my anorexia days, after my husband had passed away, but I was at least grateful that my chances of lung cancer were less than theirs. Meanwhile, with Mimi sitting next to her on her towel, watching and learning, Amanda continued to cause a sensation with the local male population wherever she went. The telephone rang nonstop and cars cruised slowly past the house, with one young man even strumming his guitar and singing about her attributes from the safe distance of the road.

My neighbours, the Two Ladies, finally plucked up the courage to pay a visit, asking a favour that I found difficult to refuse: they wanted to use my land for an organic vegetable patch. The small strip of earth that surrounded their house was woefully inadequate. If I would agree, they wanted to prepare the soil for autumn planting. 'I hope that you plant according to the phases of the moon,' I quipped. Their two well-trained little dogs sat patiently at their feet as Catherine and Geneviève gave each other that look of pure complicity that takes years of understanding to build. Funnily enough, they explained, it was scientifically proven to be the only way to garden.

Did everyone in this area have such far-reaching knowledge? Didier the plumber knew and understood women and machinery. Claire was the unwritten authority on anything and everything from natural disasters, spot removal and personal relationships to education (specialising in mathematics, history and French verb conjugations), upholstery and anything mechanical or electrical. Sylvie Goyénèche, my friend from Apt, could whip up a delicious three-course meal for family and friends with the most basic ingredients and costing next to nothing. The other string to her bow was veterinary science, having worked as a show dog judge for over twenty years. And now there were the Two Ladies. Catherine had an encyclopaedic knowledge of anything botanical as well as veterinary science, while Geneviève seemed to excel only in dog and cat walking — though I was sure that there was some craft or skill that she was keeping well hidden from me. Everyone appeared to be experts in areas where I had little or no skills, so I felt that it wasn't my place to mention that before they put so much time and effort into tilling the soil, I would have put up some sort of barrier to keep out marauding foxes and other beasties that might come across the land.

Meanwhile, the ground needed to be prepared, weeded and fertilised, and the Two Ladies were always available to stay for lunch. The extra long extensions on the table remained fully extended, tablecloths washed and folded ready for the next meal and plates stacked high, while delicious aromas wafted from the barbecue as Raymond delighted in burning the sausages, saying that was an Australian tradition. The Two Ladies wanted to display their knowledge of wine: the whole process, from A–Z. Raymond explained to them that when it came to wine, Australians were impressed not with the provenance nor the year of the bottle, but with the quantity that you could guzzle. The empty plates with greasy smears would arrive beside the dishwasher waiting to be stacked, washed and unloaded ready for the next meal.

Summer was nearly finished and soon it would be time for everyone to go home. Amanda had tested me to the limit when she spilt a full glass of red wine across the keyboard of my laptop. All the wonderful work that she had done during the summer was ruined as the computer lay inert and ruined in the workshop of the computer specialist in Avignon. She had killed it, and I wanted to do the same to her. In September, Mimi would be starting her first year of secondary schooling in Apt, while Harry was motivated and ready to start back at his school in the village. It was definitely time for the children and me to be alone together.

Following one of our long leisurely lunches, I heard a tell-tale creak from the back door. From the kitchen window, I could see Amanda's lithe brown legs sticking out from behind the gas reservoir. I caught sight of a cigarette in one hand, a glass of rosé in the other.

'Amanda, you are smoking next to a huge gas container. Are you completely mad? Your parents will not be pleased when I have to ship your body parts back to them. I think it is time that we had a talk.'

The gas company was coming the following week to fill the empty reservoir, but Amanda was none the wiser. Australia-bound at last, with her newly acquired honey tan and Scandinavian blond highlights, she teetered under the weight of her cumbersome backpack, ready to face the challenges of being a smart young thing around her home town of Melbourne.

CHAPTER NINE

Right Before Your Eyes

Summer was over and Raymond's visit too. For a change, his return flight was leaving from Rome, and it didn't take much for us all to be convinced that a week's family holiday in Rome before his flight was in order. We packed the car in record time, arranged for Sylvie, our friend and cat lover, to take the cats and we were ready. Having a business meant my freedom was severely curtailed; no longer could I grab the children and head off on a whim for a weekend by the sea. My presence was required to see new clients in to the properties, deal with suitcases that had gone astray at the airport, and begin the tedium of washing and ironing the sheets for the next lot of clients. The solution was easy. It would not break the bank if for once the sheets were sent to the laundromat and Sylvie stepped in to replace me if any problems arose. Thanks to Amanda's specialist computer tuition, I had managed to find an outstanding hotel in Rome with a last-minute deal that included parking for our car.

Rome has never been my favourite city; too big, noisy and difficult to navigate. So it was with a certain amount of trepidation that we pulled into the northern part of Rome, in the elegant Parioli area. Harry had just turned eleven and was showing signs of coming out from his sister's shadow. Tired and weary from the long drive, he said that he wanted something to eat and drink. Loading him up with money, I thought that he would go downstairs to the lobby and order something from the bar. I severely underestimated the capabilities of my child. Leaving the safety of the hotel he navigated the streets of Rome in search of a supermarket. He too, made lists:

1. *Crispy rolls.*
2. *Slices of ham, salami and cheese.*
3. *A bottle of red wine.*
4. *Fizzy drink.*
5. *Large blocks of chocolate.*

'How on earth did you make yourself understood, Harry? How did you know where to go?' Mimi was astounded that her little brother had beaten her to it.

'No one speaks English or French around here. I just followed this lady who had the same look on her face that *Maman* gets sometime. You know, really busy and panicky. She had an empty shopping basket on her arm so I knew that she would lead me to food.'

He handed Mimi one of the gigantic green crocodile sweeties that the cashier had given him for being so delightful. Harry was learning that being cute, blond and blue-eyed like his father had distinct advantages.

Our days were spent marching up and down the Seven Hills of Rome and visiting all the museums and art galleries, and our nights were spent in restaurants eating risottos, veal scallops with sage and ham and semolina dumplings served with thick tomato sauce and parmesan cheese, followed by long walks around the streets and piazzas eating chocolate chip ice creams. Raymond guided us, talking incessantly about the history and art and showing us his latest skills in epigraphy, which meant that he could read the Latin inscriptions on monuments. Raymond and I were in a tourist bubble, neatly avoiding any subject that might lead us into an adult discussion about where we were going with our lives. We both deliberately sidestepped any of the hard issues: what did it matter that we lived on different continents? I didn't want to ruin a good holiday by confronting the big questions. Our relationship seemed stronger than ever, but after our summer together I was beginning to question just how much it meant to Latin Ray and, more importantly, to me.

Slivers from our life during the day started to take on monumentally huge proportions for me during the night, as I lay beside Raymond in a disturbed slumber.

Although problems are rarely solved in the middle of the night, all good self-help books advise their readers to write lists and look at all the pros and cons of any situation. But how could you put emotions and life expectations into lists and make decisions depending on which column was longest? After all, the bottom line was that we were not married. We both had our freedom and were able to walk away at any time. I had set myself up as the perfect non-wife. After Norman passed away, I had read in a women's magazine that if a couple resided together for a certain period of time and 'the mail was sent to the same address where neither person was a lodger', it was deemed that they had entered into a de facto relationship, with all the financial complications that followed. Raymond and I had gone out of our way to sustain the most committed non-committed relationship by maintaining two households, although we slept together many nights of the week when we were in the same country. I had made a decision soon after Norman had passed away that there would be no man, no father figure and no husband to replace him on a permanent basis until I thought that I was ready and, equally importantly, until the children were ready to have someone else in our lives. I had had a good look around at the obtainable men and even those who were unobtainable — the decision was easily made. I would rather be alone and independent. Freedom was becoming more and more of a priority for me. The children had their uncles and a grandfather whom they adored as male role models. Latin Ray was my best friend and sleeping partner. He was never allowed the role of Man of the House: that belonged to me. The children admired his ability to infuriate me and to torture me with his bad behaviour and his endless capability to break important things. They also saw that he gave the family some sort of lopsided stability and brought a lot of laughter to the house, usually at his own expense.

No matter how many times I think that I have made the right choice, sleepless nights always rattle my cage. Back when I first met Raymond, we had a peculiar on-off relationship until I made the decision to move on and find someone who had similar goals to me, and I found this with Norman. We both wanted the picket fence and the two point four children, the Volvo and the house in a neighbourhood where children could play in quiet streets after school and in soccer teams on the weekend, and ballet and art classes would eat up the rest of the time. Barbecues would take place in the back yard, where the lawn had been freshly mown.

The art classes were never taken but just about everything else happened. The big gaping hole had been Norman's untimely death. Our marriage had given us both lashings of true happiness — although for too short a time. People continued to say that time would heal all wounds and very soon I would want to be with someone else and continue with my life. People had no idea what was going on in my head at night — people who slept well at night and didn't wander around aimlessly for hours at a time. People, women in particular, would give me handy hints on how to improve my emotional life, disregarding the fact that their own relationships were in a precarious state and disintegrating right before their own eyes. Older and wiser now, though still in deep shock after the death of my husband, I could see that Raymond and I shared the convenience factor rather than deep love and understanding. Having had the experience of a strong marriage, I was ruined for life; I wanted a partnership, not friendship.

After our move to France, I noticed gratefully that French women do not give advice so freely about emotional matters. However, these are the same women who spend hours musing over the correct push-up bra and matching g-string yet turn a practised blind eye to their husband's infidelities. Observing from the periphery, I came to realise that marital relationships were far more complicated than I had imagined. Good marriages that stood the test of time didn't just happen; daily nurturing was needed — a task that I felt completely incapable of undertaking at this stage. So, for the first time, it was on a happy note that I waved Raymond goodbye from Rome. It was now easier. I loved him and he loved us. Yet more than anything I wanted a full-time committed relationship; the stumbling block was that I had only ever really wanted it with my deceased husband, and that was the one thing I could never have.

~~

Heading away from Fiumicino, Rome's international airport, I started on yet another thousand-kilometre drive back to our home in France. The crack of dawn on Sunday is the best time to be on the Italian roads. Almost an hour went by without us seeing another car going in either direction. Had World War III been declared and we were the only ones who didn't know about it? It was somewhat unnerving. Large trucks are not allowed on the expressways on Sundays and the rest of Italy was either still in bed or getting ready to go to church and then sit down to the big Sunday lunch with the family. Driving up the long straight expressway heading north to France, the children sang at the top of their voices to French pop tunes blaring out from their Walkmans, while self-doubt blared in my mind.

It seems that every time we do a long-distance drive, problems that have been stewing away on the back burner are resolved one way or another. The two main areas of concern were achingly dull in their constant repetitiveness: France and Raymond. The answer was right before my eyes if only I could put everything into perspective and in order:

1. *Had I made the right decision to stay in France?*
2. *Did I know what I was doing with my business?*
3. *Would I make money or lose it? Buying the last house was a seriously bad move.*
4. *When should I start to put the properties on the market and sell up?*
5. *Why couldn't Raymond and I just break up? Surely I rated myself higher than a convenience factor in someone's life?*
6. *Shouldn't I put some effort into finding a Frenchman and go totally French?*

I had to stop berating myself for my confusion and just accept the present situation. In the end, destiny would take care of it. As far as the first question went, tickets to Sydney for the children's half-term holidays in November were already booked. Even though I had to take them out of school a week early for their holiday, it was of prime importance that Mimi and Harry knew about Australia and that they never forgot the land where they were born. They needed to be able to mimic the flat Australian vowels, understand the culture and cope at school; after all, there was no need to become totally French.

It was a tricky situation with the schools. The teachers could readily understand that my children needed to touch base with their roots and strengthen family ties but they looked at their fairly pathetic grades and continued to ask whether my experiment with the children's education was in fact working. Maybe they would be better off in an International School in Aix-en-Provence? Marseille? Or even Paris? This translated loosely as finding a school as far away from them as possible because it was proving to be extremely taxing dealing with non-French students. It also offended them that I did not want to put down long and deep roots in France, a country where I was creating a business but which obviously was not good enough to call home.

It was pointless trying to explain our needs to a teacher who had never been to Paris and rarely to Marseille. Someone who spent their holidays, over twelve weeks per year, pottering around their home and had the rare family visit in Brittany or Normandy but never ventured outside of France. The French have always argued that it is difficult travelling through Europe, continually changing currencies, but with the advent of the Euro, this argument had become dead in the water. The reality is that the French don't like going outside of France.

~~~

When November finally rolled around, our Sydney holiday got off to a wonderful start. First stop: an exhilarating swim at Manly Beach followed by a cold beer for me and some large lemonades with packets of salt and vinegar crisps for the children. The yellow and red flags were up. The beach patrol was on duty. It was a heady mix, an intoxication of all of the senses: girls in skimpy bikinis; tanned wall-to-wall muscles on young men carrying oversized Malibu boards down to the surf, with board shorts sliding off their narrow hips; the glare of the sun bouncing off the sand; the vivid colours of beach towels, hats and bags. Seagulls screeched and dive-bombed the innocents holding bags of hot chips in their hands. Sulphur-crested cockatoos and multihued rosellas had plumage that hardly seemed natural. The strange sounds, luscious tropical scents and excess of fluorescent colours hypnotised me, pulling me deeper into the familiar yet exotic landscape.

After such a blast to the senses, the three of us knew that it would be difficult to reintegrate into our lives in France. But we never guessed just how hard it would be until we arrived at Avignon railway station, exhausted and fractious because the wonderful spring weather in Sydney was no longer with us — even the normally translucent blue skies of Provence were now black and threatening. The November rains were about to begin — rains that would bring life to the crops and fill up the desperately depleted water table, giving life back to the numerous springs and creeks that abounded in the hills and across the plain of the Luberon.

During the hot summer months, we would watch in endless hope for signs of clouds along the horizon that might break the cycle of the oppressive heat. The thunder would roll past and clap into a neighbouring valley, emptying a pitiful amount of rain into the hills. November brought out the true clouds, with serious rainfall to the point of flash flooding. Nature's rhythm rarely varied. Good solid rainfall would arrive and leave us slewing around in the mud; scars from the wheels of tractors and other heavy machinery would be etched deep into the ground, and once the mud froze, there they would remain until well after Christmas. Ah, Christmas, we all sighed. No family or friends were coming to visit this Christmas. Home alone.

My friend Lizzie, whose husband Andrew had renovated my houses before I opened my business, was at the TGV station to meet us. We couldn't have thought of a better welcome as she roared with delight when we clambered from the train. When I was a young girl, 'bright and bubbly personality' meant that a young woman was encased in layers of puppy fat. Bright and bubbly was the only way to describe Lizzie — fat she was not. She always had her finger on the pulse. Her knowledge was comprehensive and far-reaching, with information garnered from the local French radio station that blared incessantly in her car. She knew about the best deals for inexpensive holidays, the deadlines for paying taxes; medical and veterinary problems did not faze her. We bundled into her car and allowed her to ferry us home. Already there was more than an autumnal chill in the air. Winter was around the corner. The trip along the RN100 more than confirmed this; the long straight main road from Avignon to Apt was a patchwork of colours, the branches of the cherry trees standing bare in the fields a strong reminder that winter was approaching.

Our senses could not cope with the differences between the two countries. The heavy salty humid air, the bright colours, the sounds, the traffic, the exotic flora and fauna, the heat rising from the pavement, the smell of grease from the fast-food outlets, the multicultural faces of Australians were only a part of our Sydney life. The city itself had changed so dramatically, with new constructions, expressways, toll ways and tunnels springing up all over. It had been hard to assimilate the infinitesimal layers and changes in a mere seventeen days. As always, the children had accepted this as their other life, quickly adopting the familiar swagger, gestures and language of young Australians. Suddenly we were back in the French countryside, empty and still — and the black threatening skies with the portent of cold and rainy days loomed over us.

Lizzie whispered into my ear that the next day she was coming to pick me up early; she had a surprise. She left us with our two small suitcases standing outside the Wild Thyme Patch. Her children, unlike mine, were finishing their school day (our holiday had been slightly longer than the half-term school break) and she was in a hurry to greet them at the school gate. I was left standing outside the house, rummaging in my pocket in a forlorn search for the house key.

Claire, my own private house fairy, had been hard at work. Our relationship had blossomed and transformed into one of huge trust and admiration. We both shared a love of excellent food and vast quantities of whisky, which we often consumed at each other's homes. She was a phenomenally industrious person, working through lunchtimes or well past the standard thirty-five hours per week if a job had to be done. Her upholstery work was immaculate, as was everything she did. This time her magic wand had been swept across our living room, which with the open fire blazing was a comforting and homey sight.

Even as we moved through the rooms, touching familiar objects and revisiting our photos on the wall, we seemed to be strangers in our own home, which was fragrant with the wonderful but still very foreign smell of the lavender-scented water that Claire used to wash the floors. The telephone broke the silence — even its ring sounded foreign and very French.

We had been down this path before. It would not take more than twenty-four hours to snap back into French mode, speaking French, eating French, being not quite French. The children needed to wash and eat. Mimi was going off on a two-night school excursion the next day to the northern area of Provence — yet again she would have to sit still, though only for a two-hour journey. My heart ached for her but it was a compulsory school trip. Claire had thought of everything and had aired her sleeping bag and washed her favourite woollens as well as her black jeans with strategic tears on the knees. Small containers stood in the fridge filled with rice salads alongside a large bowl of lettuce with baby tomatoes and a covered plate of thickly sliced ham and hard-boiled eggs; the roast chicken stood under foil, deliciously moist and tender. My job, it appeared, was to make a picnic for Mimi's lunch in the bus but more importantly to get her to school on time. As we fell heavily into our beds that night at six o'clock, my last thought was that I hoped that the alarm would ring the next day. Something buzzed at the back of my mind that Lizzie had spoken about but it was already too late. I was diving through the crashing waves in Manly, celebrating a catch at first slip with the Australian cricket team and wiping the beer foam from my upper lip. It was good to be home.

CHAPTER TEN

The Mark of Zorro

Mimi could barely drag herself out of bed the following morning; sleepy and cross, it was going to be a long day for her and her companions. Miraculously her attitude changed the moment she saw her girlfriends; throwing her sleeping bag and her small backpack into the underneath hold of the coach, she clambered on board. Our family rule for travel has always been that if you can't carry it yourself, you don't take it: clean underwear, a toothbrush and a book — the rest was superfluous.

I stood back and watched the procession of young girls from her class weave between the cars with their oversized luggage; strong, wide straps restrained the bursting suitcases. The corner of a silky red satin shirt peeked out from one ready-to-burst bag. Where and when would this outfit get an outing? I dared not think. It was only eight o'clock in the morning and already the various sets of pre-pubescent girls were

seething with high excitement, inching closer to the
edge of group hysteria. Large masticated wads from the
endless sticks of chewing gum shoved between their
glossed lips gave them the vacuous appearance of cows.
Their hair, which they had spent the previous evening
and the best part of the early morning plaiting into
small braids entwined with coloured thread and beads,
fell across their sleep-creased faces in the luxurious silk
curtains that young girls have only briefly before they
start on a course of destruction with the bleach bottle.

The boys were standing around looking
uncomfortable with their bodies and the situation;
given half the chance they would stay at home with
Maman and the television remote control. They
clambered onto the coach steps, deliberately
overbalancing as a last show of devilment for their
parents' benefit. Young expectant faces turned towards
the beaming parents for a final wave before they
collapsed together in a heap of laughter and silent farts
onto the floor. The teachers were already raising their
eyes towards the heavens, hoping for the courage that
would see them through the next seventy-two hours
without submitting the main ringleaders to a slow and
violent death. I could stand back and wave my daughter
off knowing she was in the safe hands of several strong-
minded teachers, glad that it was their chosen
profession and no longer mine. The one time that I
been in charge of a group of giggling schoolgirls on a

ski camp had maimed me for life. Fifteen years later, I still could not raise my hand to volunteer as a parent-helper on any school excursion.

Seats were taken. The head count checked. The first-aid kit checked and loaded into a compartment behind the driver. Monsieur Gallegos, the headmaster, who was always highly visible at every school function, was the last to get on the coach to give some final words to the students about carrying the school name and, of course, their own with pride. All systems were ready to go and with a honk of the coach's horn, off they set. I wasn't even sure why — or more importantly exactly where — they were going for the next seventy-two hours. Lizzie was nearby, signalling me over to her. She was busy dabbing her eyes with a tissue while waving to her son. I couldn't even think about missing Mimi, I could only concentrate on the state of my stomach. It felt like dinnertime. I was either ravenous or exhausted, I couldn't tell which. Seventy-two hours earlier we had been eating spicy laksa in the steaming heat of Singapore. The signals were confused. Curse bloody jet lag.

'Hen, are you ready? Is something the matter with your foot? Why are you still wearing your slippers?'

I looked down at my footwear balefully; at least I had managed to change out of my pyjamas.

'Lizzie, pick me up from my house in ten minutes. I'll go home and put on my shoes.' The aroma of freshly baked, hot bread was wafting out of the nearby bread shop, dragging me towards it like a magnet. Through my jet-lagged confusion, my brain could just compute 'hunger then shoes'. The first of the heavy drops of rain started to fall. Later in the day I would be grateful that the first appropriate winter footwear found at the bottom of the cupboard had been my sturdy, waterproof hiking boots. Punctual as always, Lizzie arrived precisely ten minutes later, and while she explained where we were going I started devouring slices of roast chicken on a baguette still warm from the oven, with mayonnaise and lettuce squeezing from the bread onto my chin and dropping onto my coat.

'Fasten your seat beat. We're off to Valréas.'

'Why?'

As the Wild Thyme Patch receded into the distance and the rain drops became increasingly heavy on the windscreen, I mulled over what possible reason she could have to go on a two-hour drive and why I had to come along.

'Dogs. Little dogs. Well, puppies really. Truffle dogs — no, I mean truffle puppies. I saw an ad for some black labrador puppies that have been weaned on truffle oil to make them truffle dogs. I want to buy one for Andrew as a Christmas present.' My mouth gaped open. For the best part of four months the children had been continuously harping on about their need for two labradors: one white, one black. Names had been picked out, discussed and changed on a daily basis. We had come very close to getting one from a litter in June but the gods were smiling on me and the opportunity passed by. But I could feel certain doom approaching with the driving rain that was now falling in hammering sheets. Visibility was nil. The little snippets of the scenery that I could see did not look like our countryside in the Luberon. We were now in serious winegrowing country. No matter which direction I swivelled my head, the rolling hills were deep green. No bunches of purple grapes were left on the vines, which were still swathed in green leaves — whose days were numbered because of the sudden drop in temperature; winter was approaching earlier than predicted.

We found the supermarket car park on the outskirts of the town — our designated pick-up stop. Lizzie fished in her bag for the telephone number to announce our arrival. Within five minutes, a silver Renault was flashing its headlights at us. We were to follow the driver to his house.

'Stop. This is really mad. I don't like it. We are following some man to his house; no one knows where we are; we are in the middle of nowhere; I can't even read the street signs, it's raining so hard; and worse still my telephone has no signal in this area. What if he is a madman or an axe murderer?'

Nothing but nothing was going to stop Lizzie getting a truffle dog for her husband for Christmas.

'Come on. Safety in numbers. I am sure that he is a family man and they will be lovely people.'

Lizzie always believed that good reigned in the world and people would be lovely.

And of course they were. This family adored labradors and had bred many litters from their champion truffle-finding male. The puppies had been weaned on the highly addictive smell and taste of oil infused with truffles, which had been dabbed liberally and frequently on their tongues. As the puppies grew, they played a game of finding the sock soaked in truffle oil that had been well hidden behind objects in the shed; as they grew wiser and older, the game was made harder and harder. The owner showed us how to play the game with little pieces of truffle that looked more like rabbit droppings than something that one would pay a fortune for in restaurants.

There were only two dogs left in the litter: two black males. Two gorgeous black puppies falling around helplessly, sweet, adorable. Did my children really need a dog? I looked at the parents of the litter; the bitch and the male were alert, strong and full of personality. We picked up the puppies to inspect them for any signs of weakness or malformation. Definitely. Absolutely. No question about it. The children and I needed a dog. I took out my chequebook and signed away vast sums in the belief that this dog would turn out to be a terrific guard dog, a best friend for the children, a great reason for long walks, and in his spare time he would look for truffles, dropping them at my feet for *Maman* to put into yummy runny omelettes — even though nobody in the house really liked eggs — and other wonderful French truffle dishes that I would look up in my cookery books.

It was up to Lizzie to choose which puppy suited Jet, the name that her children had chosen. Pointing the finger at the hyperactive jet-black puppy, her decision was made. The other puppy, which had a violent white flash down his chest, was coming home with me. We set off through the driving rain and now fading light; neither of us had thought to bring along some sort of cage or large cardboard box to carry Jet home. Neither of us had dreamt that we would be taking home two puppies, and soon they were in the process of rolling from one side of the car to the other. The swaying of the car and the sudden change in environment had a disastrous loosening effect on their bowels.

At the service station we cleaned the car up as best we could and patted the dogs into a slumber that we hoped would last most of the drive. Had I been awake I would have heard Lizzie fuming all the way home at her pathetic friend who, like the puppies, had found the experience utterly exhausting. But I, too, fell asleep and snored with the puppies all the way down the expressway back to Apt.

Harry and I couldn't wait to show Mimi the new member of our family, who had temporarily been called Flash or Nelson Mandela; mostly he was called Nopuppy or Puppyno. The coach was due back outside the school the next day at five o'clock. As always, Monsieur Gallegos was there to meet and greet the parents and the coachload of very subdued, exhausted children. They could barely stagger down the steps, having had a long road trip and next to no sleep in the past seventy-two hours.

As always Lizzie was there on time, divine little Margaux standing at her side holding the lead of their new dog, Jet. In sharp contrast, I was running late, dishevelled and panicky. I watched from across the road as the blond head of Lizzie's younger son Ollie stuck out from the group of boys squeezing through the door of the coach. He swept up the new puppy, squealing with delight and pulling Margaux's pigtails playfully. His family all rejoiced at his safe return. Margaux jumped up and down, unable to contain her excitement about the new puppy. Lizzie's older son Louie stood to one side, away from his siblings, and even from across the road I could see that he was putting on his 'Older Mature Brother Look', something that he had been working on; now in the early throes of adolescence, he had recently perfected it. Little bread rolls stuffed with chocolate appeared miraculously from Lizzie's backpack, only to be wolfed down in one bite by her children. I was woeful in my inability to be punctual or to produce afternoon snacks from my handbag. I could not cut myself in two and pick up Harry from his school, whip down to the bread shop to buy wonderful afternoon snacks and then battle through the afternoon traffic jam that brought Apt to a complete ten-minute standstill with the release of 2000 public school students, many of whose parents double-parked illegally along the road while ten or more coaches perched hazardously at the exit of the high school, all in readiness to carry them away to their afternoon's destinations.

As she absorbed the fact that her best friends had got the black labrador puppy that both she and Harry had been wanting, the crestfallen look on Mimi's face only lasted a few seconds, but for me it was an eternity. Lizzie always had cats wandering all over the house — now they would have the most wonderful black puppy. Unlike me, Mimi never seethed with jealousy; full of sweetness and good humour, she laughed with her friends at their new black-nosed baby, poking out from Margaux's jacket.

'Hey, *Maman*, bet you're glad that it's not us cleaning up puppy poo all over the house.'

Harry could no longer control himself and cried out:

'She didn't have the time. *Maman* had a meeting at the bank and then she had to pick me up and then come back down here to Apt to meet you at school. She didn't have the time to go back home to get our dog. Mims, we've got the matching dog at home. We're going to call him Sambo, Prince or Nelson Mandela. He's Jet's brother.'

Mimi and Harry were leaping around for joy, and within one minute I had made the wonderful transition from the Worst Mother in the Whole World to the Best. They understood that things were hard financially and that because I was a single mother concessions had to be made, but a pet had been long overdue and finally I had come through with the pet of their dreams. Already he was showing the hallmarks of being the dog of my nightmares, staining every carpet with large soggy puddles and chewing his first little leather lead in half. Little did I realise then that it was only the beginning.

By the time we reached home, we had made a family decision that the name Sambo was politically incorrect. Standing in front of the puppy, it was obvious that he should be called Zorro because of the white flash down his chest. All other names suddenly seemed foolish and inappropriate.

So Zorro came into our lives and proceeded on his path of destruction. It was the first time that I would take over sole responsibility for an animal. During the course of my childhood, my sister and I had had several dogs, but living with a dog and looking after one are completely different things. Kate and I would occasionally walk the dog to the end of the road but most times that was put off until later. It was lucky that the animal did not depend on us, as we often forgot to give it food and water.

Another yoke was around my shoulders, and this time round I knew that I was going to be responsible for the animal day and night. The matter was taken firmly in hand and I told the children that under no circumstances would this animal be an inside dog. He was a working animal — a very expensive truffle dog that belonged outdoors in his very expensive new kennel in the courtyard next to my bedroom. Zorro made himself at home, and the courtyard was soon strewn with bristles from the outdoor broom and the pinecones that had been carefully stacked in a basket ready for the fire.

All my good intentions went down the drain the moment Zorro started to whimper at night. Having spent a large portion of my life battling insomnia, I have become a very light sleeper and jump up wide awake at any unusual noise or light. Zorro cried and whimpered. I cried and whimpered when I saw that he had been chewing my mobile telephone, and my cries turned to a howl when I realised that he had eaten the end off the cordless telephone. I put a clock under his blankets but this too was chewed. He was inconsolable. I should have known then and there that I couldn't win this battle. I should have sent up the white flag and given up the fight but I was determined to outsmart and outwit this tiny puppy. I had managed to raise two children by myself — admittedly both children slept in my bed with me for many years until one night they both got up and said that they were going to their own beds and I would have to cope by myself through the night. My theory had been that children don't sleep with their parents forever, so sooner or later, between the ages of one and eighteen, they eventually leave the marital bed and find that having their own space is better than being with their parents. I was not going to replace them with a snuffling puppy. Absolutely not. Out of the question.

At the end of the first week, I was a complete and utter wreck. Everything in the house of any value had teeth marks or had been completely ruined; the automatic unlocking device on the car key, the remote control for the television, all of our pens — even his beautiful expensive kennel had parts ripped off it. I spent the best part of the night patting the puppy to sleep and then listening to him howl, whimper and cry pathetically the rest of the night. I was holding firm, even though the temperature was now falling lower and lower. Zorro was cold and miserable and wanted me to rescue him. Little did he realise that we had very little heating in the house and that during the night, after the open fire died out it was marginally warmer outside.

We continued to shower Zorro with love. From the safety of Sydney, Raymond gave me advice on how to assert my authority as the master with a rolled-up newspaper, tapping him gently but firmly on his rump, maintaining consistent boundaries that he could not overstep. I rolled out the white flag and proceeded to send it up the pole. The dog had won this round. We did not have a nice laundry with washable floors and central heating for him to sleep in like his brother Jet, who slept peacefully next to the radiator and sometimes had to be woken up and reminded to go outside to do his business, having slept heavily all night. I was ready to ask Dr Clément for a sedative from his medical bag either for me or for Zorro but our telephone only worked intermittently after Zorro had sunk his little teeth into it.

After a fortnight, I realised that I had made one of the most monumentally expensive mistakes of my life. The list of objects that Zorro had eaten, chewed, destroyed, annihilated was growing daily. The Two Ladies were purple with anger when they saw that Zorro had been looking for truffles in the vegetable plot — ten weeks of hard work destroyed. I was contemplating my options while looking up dog obedience classes in the Yellow Pages. To match her perfect-looking children, husband and life, Lizzie now had the perfect dog. Jet could sit on command and was already completely house-trained. Was it true that dogs resemble their masters? Did this mean that I was chaotic and uncontrollable?

Mon petit — my little darling — was rapidly growing bigger, and something needed to be done about him as soon as possible. Harry was at morning school on Saturday while Mimi, as a high school student, attended school only four days per week, Wednesday being a day off for sport and music and other activities. She took advantage of both Wednesday and Saturday to sleep in until nearly midday.

One Saturday morning I noticed that Zorro's familiar yelps had turned into something that sounded seriously wrong. Zorro had stuck his head through the black wrought iron gate of the courtyard. He was completely wedged and becoming more distressed by the minute. The little red bandanna that he sported around his neck instead of a collar had become entangled in the lacy wrought iron and was holding him fast. He was wriggling and squirming. I cut the bandanna free but that did not solve the problem: his head was stuck through one of the holes and there was no way that I was able to push it back. Panic was rising as I called out to Mimi for help.

Emergency numbers flooded my brain from television: Was it '000' or '999' or '911' or '17', '18' or '19'? I rang the fire brigade on '18'. They answered promptly, asking what the nature of the problem was, who was speaking and from where.

'It is *mon petit* — he has his head stuck between the holes in the wrought iron gate.'

'Calm down, *madame*. You must remain calm. How old is he? Stay with him. Go and open the gates to your property because the firemen are already in the car and they will be there shortly. Do not panic, *madame*. Help is on its way.'

The people in the main square of Apt for the busy Saturday markets looked up as the red truck, with every light flashing and siren squealing, rushed towards St Saturnin les Apt. I could see the flashing lights on the horizon before I could hear the cacophony of screeching brakes, truck doors slamming, sirens, raised voices and equipment being thrown in the air, all in a chorus of organised chaos. The captain rushed to my side then suddenly stopped in his tracks, a wide smile spreading across his very tanned handsome face.

'*Madame*, you did not mention that your *petit* was of the four-legged variety. I will help you with your problem but first I must call the hospital that is waiting with a paediatric team for your little son's arrival.'

The firefighters contemplated the problem. The only solution they could come up with was the large pneumatic scissors that cut through metal — usually used in extracting people from car accidents. A call was relayed back to base and the Jaws of Life were dispatched without delay.

The commotion from the firefighters and their wailing trucks brought my few neighbours running to my assistance — or rather, to see first-hand what the

mad Australian woman was up to this time. The Two
Ladies, my nearest neighbours, arrived first and I stood
back with them and watched as the firefighters tried to
comfort the puppy and work the Jaws of Life at the
same time. Zorro sprang free from his iron collar and
leapt into the arms of one of the firefighters, a woman
who by this stage had fallen under his charms and
showed little or no intention of giving him back. The
job was completed. The puppy was saved. We waved
them all goodbye, cheerful in the knowledge that this
emergency at least had a happy ending; most of their
work revolved around extricating people from cars
wrapped around trees or dragging damaged cars and
people from deep ditches. As we were saying farewell,
Mimi wandered out from the bathroom, a halo of clean
hair bouncing around her freshly washed and scrubbed
face, to see why there was so much noise. Harry walked
through the front gates after his Saturday morning at
school, shouting that he needed sustenance immediately
as he was dying from hunger, and that something
dreadful in the neighbourhood must have happened as
there were sirens and fire engines everywhere.

Disaster averted, the firefighters collected their tools,
packed their trucks and sped off down the road back to
their control centre in Apt, leaving a trail of red dust
rising through the dense grapevines. Mimi showed her
brother how the dog had managed to become stuck fast
in the gate. Catherine, the younger of the Two Ladies,

inspected the lacy wrought iron gate and told me that she would find some thin wire and lattice that could be fixed onto the gate to prevent Zorro repeating his actions.

'Ah, Catherine, I think that you underestimate my puppy. As if he would do that again. He might be young but he is not stupid.' To my horror, Zorro was at that moment in the process of shoving his head through another hole in the gate. I shook my head: just as well he was a first-class truffle dog because his behaviour was quite idiotic.

While Catherine went off to find the lattice and the thin wire, our neighbour from the other side arrived. Bernard Blanc lived with his wife and their two grown-up daughters in a house that we could see in the distance from our front verandah, across a very large fallow field. One of his daughters was in high school and she and Mimi would walk along the country lane together to the bus stop at the end. Bernard, too, had come to investigate why we suddenly had several firefighters and their trucks on the property, especially as there was no evidence of the house burning down.

'Madame Taylor, a little word in your ear, if you have a moment.'

I went over to Bernard and shook his extended hand. This very gesture showed that I knew how to conduct myself with him: strictly formal, using surnames to address each other, shaking hands as a formality rather than the three kisses to the cheeks that was the norm here in Provence. It went without saying that I would use the very formal '*vous*' form to address him — always best to be too formal rather than too intimate. The '*tu*' form is used for best friends, family, children and animals. After a decent period of at least ten years, as neighbours we might adopt a slightly more friendly form of address, but we would remain formal for a very long time.

Though he was clearly slightly agitated, Bernard had waited patiently as the courtyard emptied of firefighters, trucks and the Two Ladies. When we were alone he began explaining what he really wanted.

'Truffles, Madame Taylor. I think that you are sitting on a very large truffle farm.' This could not be possible. The previous owners had never mentioned anything about this and it would have been a huge selling point if they had known. Monsieur Blanc proposed that later that afternoon he would come with his two truffle-sniffing dogs and they would work the property. Bernard explained that the truffle, a mass of fungus that grew underground and looked uncannily like a dried dog turd, needed water in the early autumn followed by warmth to nurture it underground until early December, when it would be ready to be unearthed and thrown into delicacies ranging from humble omelettes and *salades* to more exotic meat dishes — just in time for Christmas.

I had read about truffle hunts in magazines and books on Provence but never in my wildest dreams had I thought that I would be lucky enough to go truffle hunting — let alone on my own property. I was jumping from foot to foot. All my Christmases had come at once. The children were over the excitement of the firefighters being at the house and were now installed in their bedrooms trying to wade through the hours of homework that had to be completed by Monday morning. They had no intention of wandering through the dense and unkempt undergrowth that had a tight grip on most of the so-called garden for yet another 'French Experience', as the children mimicked, writhing in mock pain and agony. The temperature had plummeted and the Mistral had picked up, howling down from the north at ninety kilometres per hour. They called out to me that they would rather stay indoors even if it meant doing their homework.

Zorro and I greeted Bernard at the gate of the Wild Thyme Patch. My vanity had got the better of me and I had decided to forgo a sensible woollen bonnet or hat. Bernard, a true Provençal, knew better and had come equipped with his woollen headband around his head; tufts of slightly grey hair escaped its mooring. His all-weather coat covered many layers of thick sweaters, giving him a lumpy appearance. His eyes were swivelling around, unable to contain the joy that he shared with his dogs, which were salivating with excitement. Bernard's two funny-looking dogs were both highly trained truffle dogs that he had coached since birth. The chaos that ensued with Zorro meeting them for the first time was hilarious. With the three dogs running around and sniffing, barking and generally having a wonderful play, it was evident that not much work would be done. Five minutes later, we dispatched Zorro inside so that serious work could begin.

Bernard was wearing a peculiar suede leather bag strapped diagonally across his chest. He lifted up the top flap and asked me to smell the contents within. I couldn't describe what it smelt like but there was that initial rush to the senses that makes you quickly addicted. Next his 'girls', the dogs, were allowed their turn. They remembered that distinctive scent. They knew what their master wanted from them. They tore back and forth in large zigzags across the back section of the property where the oak trees had been planted many years before, then one of them gave a sudden frantic yelp and a bark, calling her master to come quickly. The girls were busy scratching the ground and putting their muzzles to the earth; they started digging frantically to their goal.

I couldn't believe it. Wasn't it meant to take hours of careful walking and deciding where to look? Obviously these dogs had seen the treasure map before; it struck me as strange that Bernard could direct them to the back of the garden and within ten minutes they had struck gold. Clods of earth were flying up everywhere. The soil was rich, black and friable. The dogs suddenly stood still, barking incessantly in case the truffle moved, which of course it would not. Bernard bent down and dug with his hands until he pulled out a small black nugget, patting both dogs on the head and talking to them in low undulating tones — he was proud of his girls. They needed a reward for their good work. A little dry dog biscuit was pulled from a pocket. Bernard shook the excess soil from his hands and continued to talk in low whispers to the dogs.

The entire property was unfenced, which was a worry now that we had Zorro the Wonder Dog. Bernard explained to me some basic rules about truffles:

1. *Never admit where you found them.*
2. *Never share with anyone else (except neighbours).*
3. *Truffle dogs need to be trained for years before they hit their potential.*
4. *Unfenced land meant that hunters for animals and truffles could 'accidentally' come onto my property, reaping the rewards.*

The dogs lay down in a heap, exhausted from their flurry of activity, while Bernard showed me some of the delights and mysteries of my property. There was bark missing from many of the trees at a height of about two

metres, which he said was from deer rubbing their
newly formed antlers. The soft earth behind the
tumbling-down garden shed at the end of the property
exposed a mass of prints that did not belong to my cats.
Bernard pointed out a clear two-pronged hoof mark: it
was obvious that the prints belonged to wild boars that
had foraged for roots and other food in the rich soil.
They too were looking for truffles. He asked if I realised
that I was also sitting on a very large subterranean water
table. This was liquid gold, as I had quickly worked out
during our first hot summer. All I needed was a deep
bore hole drilled down to it. The severe lack of water
was an increasing problem for everyone, so those who
had it were truly blessed. Gripping me by the hand and
staring maniacally into my eyes, Bernard told me that
we were excellent neighbours. He had the hunting skills
and the dogs, while I had the truffles on my land: a
perfect combination. The truffles from the first search
would be solely for me and from then on, we would
share fifty-fifty. It sounded like a wonderful idea. We
shook hands and continued with the search. I made a
mental note to find out how much it would cost to
fence a hectare of land. That would have to be my
Christmas present. There was always the slim possibility
that Zorro would find such a trove of truffles that it
could pay for the fencing.

As he was leaving, Bernard whispered to me softly that
there were other spots high up in the hills behind the

village where he knew consistent areas for growing truffles. If I would like, one day during the Christmas holidays we could even take his guns and hunt some wild boar. Although hunting and shooting was a solitary sport and certainly not one for women, Bernard was prepared to show me some of the delights of Provence that the average tourist would never see.

'You know, Bernard, I am not exactly a tourist. I may not be French but I am planning to live here for a very long time.' I felt that I had to correct his misconception.

'Madame Taylor, no matter how long you live here, no matter how proficient your French is, you will never be anything but a tourist for the people around here. Likeable, admittedly; an extremely hard worker, granted; but it takes generations to become a real Provençal. For example, look at the way you stack your wood; you don't even put it under cover. The plants you have planted in the garden are very pretty but they will not survive the winter. Please do not let me start on your dog. He lives and sleeps inside the house; he isn't trained to heel or sit, and no wonder — one minute you speak to him in English and the next in French. He digs in your vegetable garden. Who would want baby carrots with tooth marks? Do you understand how rich that plot of land is? You could grow anything. Instead of a huge crop of vegetables you have planted a large gas cylinder.'

He muffled a laugh and a snort of derision.

'No. In short, you are very nice but not wise, *n'est-ce pas?* I have watched the plumbers digging holes and draining the pond. It breaks my heart that you have no idea.'

I was dumbfounded that he held me in such contempt.

'I don't understand why you have never said anything to me before. Why did you not come here and tell me where the water was on the property?'

'You see, *madame,* that is the Provençal way. We keep to ourselves. Your business is yours and mine is mine. I will keep my word and take you truffle hunting or mushroom gathering when the time is right but you will always remain a tourist.'

My next question was about my dog, and already I was getting prepared for the reply, which did not surprise me. How to train the dog? What to do with him? Now I had allowed the dam to break open. There was no stopping Bernard: he was going to tell me everything that I had done wrong. Zorro was a very headstrong male dog that needed a strong male presence to dominate him. I had made a very poor choice in the animal; as a woman I would have great difficulties training one like him. His advice was to take the dog back to the breeders and get a full refund — again he snorted. I should have taken a female dog and chosen a breed much smaller and less trouble. I nodded my head in agreement. Deep down in my heart, I knew that Zorro was not destined to become a highly trained truffle dog. As I went inside to the warmth of the fire, I could see that Bernard was right. There was Zorro with his head stuck inside a cereal box, hitting his head on the floor trying to remove it.

That night as I lay in bed with the strong Mistral wind howling and licking at the windows, I wished that I had taken more notice of things like double glazing for windows and the state of the shutters on the house before signing on the dotted line. (It was only many years later, when the time came to do some renovations on our family home, that I discovered the true extent of the problems, such as the complete lack of insulation in the walls and roof.) This night, the violent and turbulent wind descended from Lyon down the Rhône Valley until it reached Marseille, taking a short cut across the Luberon. It was finding a way through every crack and pushing against every pane of glass of our home. No wonder the houses built in the true Provençal manner turn their backs to the north and have only minute windows.

Apart from the howling wind, there was something not quite right in the house in the middle of the night; pulling my fluffy white dressing gown around me tightly, I went to investigate. There was no evidence of smoke, gas or other lethal vapours. The children were in their beds fast asleep in some dream-filled land. For a nice change the puppy was sound asleep. I had finally conceded that it was too cold to let him sleep outdoors, so a little bed made from a cardboard box, already well chewed, had been made up in front of the fire. I went to the kitchen to make a cup of tea and that's when it hit me.

A remarkable scent was wafting from a ceramic bowl piled high with truffles, most the size of large walnuts. That afternoon Bernard had been beside himself with glee, insisting that I had the entire crop, but I could see him calculating a visit before Christmas to ensure that his family, too, had the joy of truffles in the stuffing, in the sauces or in the salad. The odour was overwhelming, a full-frontal attack on the senses. I had never experienced anything that was so exotic, so romantic, and so unbelievably addictive. The thought of going back to bed was out of the question. Water was boiled for the tea and cookery books were sought from the shelves. I spent the best part of the night sitting in the kitchen breathing in the delicious nutty perfume while reading through French recipes to see how I was going to use my little nuggets.

CHAPTER ELEVEN

Joyeux Noël 2002

Yet again, Christmas was already giving me more grief than pleasure. It would just be the three of us, as nobody in the family was able to drag themselves from the Sydney summer: the champagne sparkling water, the fine sand, the long hot summer days, the cricket and the wonderful array of tropical fruit in season. Life at the Wild Thyme Patch just couldn't compete. Our days were short, the temperature was plunging, the heating non-existent; in brief, the only thing that I could use to entice family or friends over for a quick stay were our elusive truffles and nobody was convinced that something that looked so odd was worth travelling for more than twenty-four hours in a plane to try. When Claire invited us to join their Christmas festivities, we gratefully accepted. Claire's house was up the hill from St Saturnin les Apt, set in the middle of a cherry orchard. Mimi and Harry squealed with delight. Going to Claire's meant that at least there would be another child the same age, and that meant fun in anyone's language.

The children were all on holidays and were ready to go to the Christmas market that brought Apt to a standstill every year. I had thought about travelling to the north of France to visit the world-famous Christmas markets in Strasburg but this year I needed to cut as many financial corners as possible. Diesel prices were constantly going up and a long car trip to northern France to look at a market when we had a divine one on our own doorstep in Apt just didn't make sense. No travel for us at the moment. I would deal with the financial problems first thing in the New Year.

Apt was decked out from head to foot in Christmas lights. During the weeks leading up to Christmas the council workers were up and down cranes, installing the kilometres of tiny lights that would be the showpiece of the town's Christmas decorations. Already it was looking spectacular. The tall column in the centre of the main square had lights covering the entire structure, and they then spread out across the square in a canopy of lights and shapes. Everywhere was decked out in lights. The busy market town had come alive, and instead of looking slightly tawdry and tacky, it had taken on a sleek and upbeat look. In the middle of the main roundabout was a 400-year-old olive tree alongside three cypress trees — a Provençal tradition representing welcome. Large urns had been placed discreetly at the base of the trees, holding yet more Christmas lights. The locals often remarked with pride that the lights were made in France and graced not only monuments large and small across France — not forgetting all of the Parisian monuments, in particular the Eiffel Tower — but also several big shopping centres in America, Europe and the Middle East. It was extraordinary the way in which the Christmas lights flooded the town with joy, changing it from a little country town to one that made your heart sing with happiness and pride. In Sydney, an excess of fireworks had become the traditional way of rejoicing a celebration: the Millennium, the Olympics and the New Year. Every year, they became ever more successful in painting the inky-black skyline. The effect was outstanding but short-lived, as the Sydney City Council battled tightening budget restrictions.

There was something magical about driving through Apt every night of the week when the lights were sparkling and rushing down in cascades of moving, coloured luminosity. People were tending to return to their summer habits, drinking a small aperitif at the end of the working day in the main square in order to take full advantage of the magnificent display.

～～

The main parking area in Apt had been reduced to a bare minimum as the oversized marquee was erected for the Christmas market. Inside there were stalls selling their wares: turkeys, capons (the very large castrated roosters) and free-range corn-fed chickens; lavender honey; wines; oils; olives; *fois gras*; snails in cans, ready to be served in pre-washed shells with lashings of hot garlicky butter; *fougasse à l'huile* (a delicious soft oily bread); *fruit confit* (citrus fruits, slices of melon and figs conserved and dried in a heavy sugar syrup); *calisson* (a heavy sugary fruit paste rolled into lozenges and covered in a glossy white sugar layer); dried or fresh floral decorations with Christmas candles squeezed in between the flowers and leaves; scented soap bars or large bottles of Marseille liquid soap; decorations for the house; and *santons*, or figurines. The *santons* took up a vast section of the marquee. They were available in all sizes, depending on the size of your crèche. There was a selection of standard Mary, Joseph and Baby Jesus and Three Wise Men figurines, but in order to personalise your crèche there were also farmyard animals and figures representing all the trades and parts of daily life. There were little stables to house the animals and little alcoves and shops for the tradesmen, and pastimes ranging from the basic butcher, baker and candlestick maker to the less well-known ones such as the stick gatherer for the baker's oven or the men playing cards. There were mini pumps so that you could have a running stream or a miniature fountain, diminutive trees and shrubs, fake grass and moss and different types of outbuildings to add interest to the scene. Everything had to match in size to give the correct perspective. The prices matched the size, so the stand selling the thumbnail-size animals and figures was three people deep. Mimi and Harry hopped from foot to foot begging to have our own crèche. Small economies had to be made and it was starting here.

Claire and Raphaël were in the thick of the throng, fighting their way to the front of the stall so that Raphaël could choose another animal or something else to add to their collection. Their crèche had come out of its box and was ready to be installed somewhere in the house. This year, they had decided that it would be set on the side of a hill, and shoeboxes were at the ready to be cut and carved into shape. They had been up into the hills behind our village to gather a selection of small rocks, twigs, berries, moss and lichen and a small bag of earth. The moss and lichen would cover the cardboard, and once placed in the panorama, the small pebbles would be miniature boulders.

That afternoon, Raphaël and the children went looking for more small stones and boulders to serve as the foundation for his crèche. Claire and I were in the garage stowing things away; more precisely, she was stowing while I was sitting daydreaming about Raymond. Holding a mirror in my hand, I could only think of Tennyson's Lady of Shalot. The fair damsel lived on an island just upstream from Camelot, removed from the rest of the world, and spent her days staring at the outside world with the aid of an enchanted mirror, then weaving these images into a tapestry. Sir Lancelot's arrival on the riverbank made the fair lady look at him without her mirror, thus causing it to crack from side to side, releasing a fatal curse. How many parallels could I draw between us? I lived on my own little island in the middle of France looking at life through my romantic prism, far removed from family, friends and Australia, and my impressions of people and life were distorted. My head was swimming in confusion. Claire called my name sharply, bringing me back from my momentary reverie, asking me to hand her the mirror that was beside me. But it slipped from my grip, cracking from side to side. I stared in total horror at the shards of mirror that surrounded me on the ground.

'Claire, that mirror is going to bring me seven years' bad luck.'

'Don't be so silly. This is excellent.' Scooping up one of the largest slivers, she found some fragments that she could work into the tiny crèche that this year was taking on mammoth proportions with Mimi and Harry's help.

'This year we want a babbling brook trickling down the hillside and Raphaël would like it to end up in a lake beside the manger. These pieces of mirror will be ideal. The rest we will use in decorations.'

I was not sure how she was going to incorporate broken shards of glass into Christmas decorations but Claire would find a way to work her magic. If only magic could fix my heart.

~~~

Since September 11's terrorist attack in New York, the world had been reeling in shock. At the beginning of 2002, the US launched Operation Anaconda to destroy al-Qaeda and Taliban forces in Afghanistan. Retaliation came when a bomb exploded in Bali on 12 October, killing 202 people. Only a few weeks later, Chechen rebels took 800 people hostage in Moscow; all of the terrorists were killed, along with more than 100 of the hostages, many of them children. It appeared that every time we turned on the television there was more strife somewhere in the world. By November 2002, no one was very surprised when a message was broadcast on the al-Jazeera network extolling the Bali and Moscow attacks and threatening in no uncertain terms that more were going to rock the world.

Christmas was going to be a very quiet affair, especially with the continued talk on both French and English television of the increased fear of terrorism. The public was keenly aware and fearful of bombs in backpacks that could be detonated with the aid of mobile telephones. I cancelled my Christmas shopping trip to London because I didn't want to tempt fate. The lure of the bright lights of London and shopping for books in real bookshops was a major temptation, compared to the monthly order that we made on the Internet, but I resisted. Mimi and Harry had asked me to stay, preferring to have their mother in one piece.

Many clients who had contacted me in September and October 2002 to make bookings for summer 2003 were now not taking up my early-bird reductions. In fact, they were not taking up any offers. Even the Australians, who were extremely enthusiastic travellers, had become more concerned about personal safety and the fluctuations in exchange rates, preferring to stay close to Australian shores for their holidays. Every night I went over the projected figures; they were not looking very promising. I had seriously over-extended myself with the purchase of the Wild Thyme Patch; now with the drop in bookings for the following year, things were dire. As my financial consultant often said, the figures did not lie.

When terrorism was pushed off the front page by rampant viruses and diseases, the final nail was hammered into the coffin. Australians and New Zealanders did not want to come to Europe through potentially risky Asia; nor through America, which appeared to be equally if not more perilous. The Americans had not overcome the shock of September 11, and now with the additional fear of Bovine Spongiform Encephalopathy (BSE), or Mad

Cow Disease, they were not going to cross the Atlantic. On the English television channels we watched the English Prime Minister and his family extolling the virtues of rediscovering the rolling green dales and valleys of England as a holiday destination; the vast majority of Britain vowed to continue their love/hate relationship with France at a later date.

I was experiencing difficulties tapping into the northern European countries, as I could never seem to find the right magazines or journals to place my advertisements to coerce a new market to enjoy the beauties of Provence. Norway had been voted the best place to live in the world for the second year in a row and the inhabitants had no desire to travel so far to visit a country like France. The writing was on the wall. It would soon be over for me; probably by the end of 2003 I would be heading back to Sydney with my tail between my legs, having tried with my small business and failed. With a huge effort, I set the figures aside and tried to feel a little of the festive spirit.

Christmas in France is always celebrated at midnight on Christmas Eve, so it was no surprise when Claire asked us for drinks and dinner at nine o'clock, not eight o'clock when French dinners usually start. The three of us had eaten a small late afternoon snack to stop us from fading away with hunger, as I knew from experience that we would not be eating the main course before midnight. As I pulled the car into the beginning of the long track that led through the cherry trees, I began to understand the treat that lay ahead. The cherry trees stood in straight lines, sentries at the gate, completely bare and dormant, in a deep sleep, preparing themselves for the huge display of white blossoms in late March. The courtyard and the front of the house were decked out in party lights, glittering and shimmering in the freezing cold evening air. The sky was ink black and starless — it was too cold even for the stars to be out. Mimi called out to me in a muffled voice through the layers of woollen scarves wrapped tightly from her neck up:

'*Maman*, where are all of our presents for them? *Zut, crotte, flûte*, you've forgotten them!'

'No, my darling. It's been taken care of. Come on everyone. Let's get inside. It's freezing!'

Claire had called in the morning asking me to bring a shoe for each person as well as our presents. I had a good idea what was happening but it was still fun to play ignorant. The activity in the house was reaching fever pitch, with Claire's daughters, Géraldine and Lorélie, scurrying about carrying plates piled high in preparation for the evening's meal. We gazed in amazement at the transformation of the tiny home. Claire's house was always in immaculate order. She complained incessantly that living in the middle of a cherry orchard might be romantic and pretty but the dust and filth from the fields infiltrated every corner. Evidence of this has never been witnessed and Christmas Eve was no exception. Wonderful aromas wafted out from the room that was loosely called a kitchen but was in fact a long, large cupboard with barely enough room for the tiny stove and a sink, let alone a dishwasher. Claire and her two daughters nipped back and forth creating enough food for the nine assembled guests, all standing around with mouths watering. Behind the delicious aromas you could detect whiffs of the underlying bouquet from the floor washed with hot water and lavender oil, with the occasional hint of beeswax as you passed the highly polished wooden furniture.

The space in the living room had all but disappeared, eaten up by the extensions on the dining table, making the normal-sized crèche impossible. Instead Claire and Raphaël had managed to construct a beautiful miniature crèche at the bottom of a hill, made from shoeboxes covered in the moss, lichen, twigs and other verdure they had hunted for in the hills behind the village and decorated with boulders and stones from our garden. Mary and Joseph were huddled together in the little manger. The minuscule crib lay empty, waiting for the stroke of midnight, when Baby Jesus would miraculously make his appearance. The showstopper was the cascading stream that wound its way down the cardboard hill, ending up beside the crèche in a small lake made from shards of my broken mirror. We were mesmerised by the beauty of this fantasyland. The amount of time and care that had been put in to achieve this folly, one of which graced a corner of every Provençal household, defied belief for my two little Australians, who had been brought up with garlands of tacky tinsel and an array of garish ornaments on a tall fake Christmas tree. For the past seven years, Christmas in our home had been a time of intense emotion about their absent father and my absent husband, which never seemed to abate with the passing years. Like most children, mine wanted a swag of presents and lollies, but even at their age they could sense that I needed Christmas to pass as quickly as possible. This year, we felt that we had been transported to a magical place where our cares could be left behind.

The children disappeared to Raphaël's bedroom while the adults started the aperitifs, making a quick detour past the crèche. As the youngest member of the family, it fell to Raphaël to keep the Baby Jesus out of sight until after midnight Mass, when he was officially born and could take his rightful place in the manger. This year he had kept Baby Jesus well hidden, perched precariously in a crook of a miniature tree.

The staple pre-dinner drink in the Larmenier household was whisky, and Christmas Eve was no exception. The bottles of champagne that I had brought would be served with the dessert, if we could last that long. Arranged on large white platters was an abundance of treats: little mouth-sized morsels of puff pastry with cheese, bowls of tapenade (the thick, oily black or green olive paste), fat black olives marinated in herbs and garlic and the prerequisite bowls of grilled vegetables — some puréed into a paste and others rolled into bite-size mouthfuls. *Vogue Living* would have been proud to have photographs of the setting for their Christmas edition. For a very short moment, everything looked stylised and perfect until the guests' hands started to dart greedily into the food. A sigh of satisfaction was breathed and we started the ceremony, toasting good health and happiness, rejoicing in the reunion of a happy family and friends with healthy growing children at Christmas time.

By the time we were seated at the table I was wondering if it would ever again be possible to spend a Christmas to match this one. The table was completely swathed in a theme of white and silver: white plates, white roses and white and silver ornamental birds were perched between glass candlestick holders, small bouquets of holly and Claire's best antique linen napkins. The word 'sumptuous' did not do the table setting justice. It was always a source of envy or amazement to anyone who came in contact with Claire that she managed to achieve her famous interiors with so little money. They lived a very modest life and money was constantly tight, even now that three of the four children were young adults and living away from home — a financial emergency was always just around the corner. Since November, Claire had been working

her way through the second-hand shops, trash and
treasure days in the villages and Red Cross shops to see
if anything could be gleaned for use at Christmas time.
It had paid off, and we now admired the latest pieces of
furniture that had been scrubbed back, stripped down,
repainted several times then the paint wiped off and wax
applied. When I was with Claire on one of her many
excursions to the opportunity shop in Cavaillon, we
dragged a two-seater sofa to the truck. Claire could see
past the horror of that sofa, saying that it just needed a
bit of loving care. The amount of work and effort that
had been expended was more than incredible, right
down to changing the upholstery. Claire often said with
pride that their tiny home for three people was barely
100 square metres but it always appeared to be infinitely
larger thanks to the care and effort she took to
coordinate all the fabrics, the wall friezes and the
furniture. At Claire's home, even the smallest objects
were harmonious and colour coordinated.

The food never stopped coming out from the
kitchen: fresh salmon had been whipped into a
concoction of cream and herbs and placed in some sort
of light pancakes then assembled in a large roll; breasts
of duck had been pan-fried in olive oil and honey and
herbs; vegetables had been steamed to perfection with
large blobs of white salt-free Normandy butter
drizzling down into the bowls; the wine flowed and the
conversation was unstoppable.

It was fast approaching midnight and we still hadn't arrived at the end of the meal. The plates were cleared and new ones were handed out ready for the salad followed by the cheese platter, which consisted of a selection of goat's cheeses: some rolled in ash, some covered in herbs — in various stages of maturity ranging from the very fresh soft cheese to the hard and dry older cheese.

Patrick, twisting his very substantial handlebar moustache, gave the sign. It was time. Like good guests, the children and I took our lead from Patrick, who had leapt up from the table and was already in the process of putting on layer after layer to brace himself for the plummeting temperatures outside. We would be returning in an hour's time to open presents and sample the delights that were held in reserve for dessert. Géraldine and Lorélie had drunk very little so that they could transport everyone in cars to the neighbouring village of Villars. Richard, their twenty-year-old stepbrother, had not been trusted with this task — and with good reason. As we entered the village and queued up in the narrow street to find a parking spot, I could see that we would not be the only ones running around at midnight on Christmas Eve. And when we walked into the village hall, the reason was obvious. The living crèche had started.

Standing at the entrance of the hall, we were assaulted by noise and smells. On one side of the hall there was a temporary stall set up with animals from the surrounding farms, all braying in time. It was going to be a long night. Wisely, Claire and Patrick pushed us towards the hot wine that was on offer at the back of the hall. The crèche was spectacular, and so was the overpowering smell, with every animal from the countryside making an appearance: donkeys, chickens and roosters, dogs, pigs and cows — and in the middle of it were Mary, Joseph and the baby Jesus. This year Jesus was played by the smallest arrival in the village, a baby girl whose little pink bootees hung outside of her linen robe while her mother sucked hard on a cigarette and swigged the hot mulled wine.

On our return to Claire and Patrick's home, we were greeted with yet more magic. Parcels of all shapes and sizes wrapped up in colourful paper and ribbons surrounded the nine single shoes that we had been instructed to leave beside the chimney. The children squealed with delight as they ripped open their new treasures. We arrived home at five o'clock in the morning, barely able to drag ourselves into bed for a couple of hours' sleep before the next day's marathon on the telephone.

The real Christmas present would come with Raymond's arrival in mid-January. I promised myself that 2003 would bring a resolution to our dilemma: full commitment or a decision to break off our relationship.

CHAPTER TWELVE

Advance Australian Fare

Raymond's arrival heralded the beginning of the beautiful Provençal winter weather that is continually written up in upmarket travel magazines and sets this sliver of the south of France apart as a truly magnificent January destination. The sky was forever crystal blue and cloudless. The early mornings were frosty and crisp but by lunchtime it was often possible to consider peeling off the winter woollies and exposing small areas of white flesh to the sunlight.

Time was always limited with Raymond so family discussions at the dinner table were boisterous and lively, as Mimi and Harry talked nonstop about their activities and their school life since they had last seen him. We mulled over where we should go and what we should do during the children's February holidays: 'Italy!' everyone shouted.

Important issues about the long-term future of our relationship eased towards the back recesses of our minds. Raymond continued to seduce me with words of love, admiration and adoration. Showered daily with these words and displays of love, it became impossible to talk about breaking up. We enjoyed each other's company far too much and knew each other far too well to part. Yet again my New Year's resolution went down the drain.

As we moved towards the end of January, the decision was made that a celebration of some magnitude was in order: an Australia Day Celebration. Telephone calls were made. Lists on sticky notepaper were glued to every part of my desk as we tried to secure the maximum number of Australians for a barbecue lunch and cricket match on 26 January. Guest lists were made. Emails were sent out. An Australian couple with two young children who had stayed in Saignon over Christmas but were still travelling in France were asked via email if they would like to make a return trip and come by for the weekend festivities. They were a couple of hours away by car but the idea of eating lamingtons, pavlova, burnt sausages and lamb chops, and other shining examples of Australian cuisine, was enticing enough to lure them back.

The title of Best Drinking Buddy for Raymond belonged to Kit, who lived in Saignon. Too many times I had explained to the two inebriated fools that taxis, not me, were required for transport after a big afternoon of rugby and beer at the bar in Apt. Kit and I had lived less than ten kilometres apart in Sydney, but it wasn't until we were on the other side of the world in Saignon that our paths eventually crossed. He announced that he would arrive on his Fat Boy Harley Davidson carrying a large Australian flag, a case of Fosters and some frozen meat pies in the saddlebags. I delicately put it to his ex-wife Pam that Kit would also be attending the party and that I was not quite sure how to divide my loyalties. Pam laughed at my clumsiness, saying that although they both still lived in the Luberon their paths rarely crossed due to their work commitments. She would be delighted to see him again. After all, Pam was not about to miss a winter party; as a professional caterer, this was the only time of year when she had the luxury of socialising. As she said, she would always have a deep tenderness towards Kit, but living with him or having anything to do with his life would certainly never be on her agenda again.

My own marriage had only lasted five good years before Norman became desperately ill and then passed away. It had not given me a great deal of experience in marriage or how it works, but I could not help wondering why two people could drift apart when they were so obviously made for each other. But I was happy that they both would come, and whatever reason that they were no longer together would remain firmly locked away behind their closed doors.

Deirdre was next on the list. She originally came from a tiny town in Queensland called Goombungee, which has the dubious distinction of being known as the rural Iron Man capital, as it hosts Iron Man and Iron Woman competitions each Australia Day. Her naturally inquisitive mind, combined with years travelling with her pilot husband Geoff in the far-flung reaches of Asia and Europe, allowed her to pick up the language and cooking skills of any country. She had a working knowledge of a variety of Asian and European languages, but her strongest suit was without a doubt her cooking skills: Asian in particular. Deirdre had a secret that she shared with few people. In a moment of weakness, she confessed to me that her true claim to fame was her tap-dancing; when she paused for effect, I had held my breath and hoped that she wasn't about to say 'erotic naked tap-dancing'. With her fifties making an alarming appearance on her horizon, she had enrolled in classes in Singapore and discovered that whether she had talent or not, she adored tap-dancing — and she had continued to tap for the next eight years. Deirdre never held back with a song or a loud joke. It would not be long before this secret was exposed. Those in the know had joked in vain about a tap-dance spectacle that she should perform for family and friends, in the vain effort to edge her away from the immense depression that she was succumbing to daily as her husband lay in the hospital in Apt fighting for his life in the advanced stages of throat cancer. We all agreed that it wasn't fair; Geoff had never smoked a cigarette or a cigar in his life.

As in the majority of my relationships, I was split in two. I had a few toes of one foot in the Anglophone expatriate community, whose company I enjoyed but for the most part were in a different stage of life, whiling away their evenings with canasta and bridge. For them, afternoons filled with schoolwork problems were long gone. My other foot was firmly in the camp of the French speakers with children of similar ages to mine.

Living in France had thrown my life completely off kilter. The social skills that I had observed from a young age and assimilated almost by osmosis tended to be useless in France. I was still coming to terms with how to meet other mothers in my new world, where my expectations did not match theirs. For the French parents, it would never cross their minds to chat over endless pots of tea or go to a coffee shop after school drop-offs. It just wasn't part of their culture. There appeared to be some unwritten laws for socialising that were the same for both the local primary school and the high school in Apt. When it came to socialising with other parents, certain things were completely acceptable:

1. *To stand in the middle of the street talking and blowing smoke into pedestrians' faces.*
2. *To stand at the front door of the family home but never enter.*

3.   *To stand and chat in the middle of the aisles of the local supermarket (but not near the bread section, as you can never admit that you buy bread from the supermarket).*

4.   *To bump into each other at the market with your basket brimming with vegetables and a large plait of garlic and several stalks of leeks on view. This proves that you fall into the category of the Good French Wife and Mother.*

5.   *To telephone at lunchtime as everyone is at home while having their main meal in front of the news on television.*

6.   *To invite parents around for a glass of summer rosé — but be prepared for refusals as this would take place in your own personal domain.*

Being a non-native French speaker, I was given leeway only up to a certain point to grasp the cultural connotations. Gradually, I was coming to terms with what was completely unacceptable:

1.   *Never under any circumstance use the friendly 'tu' form for 'you'. Always address other parents as* monsieur *or* madame *— their surname is redundant as it suggests familiarity. Wait until they offer to use a slightly friendlier form.*

2.   *Never invite other parents around to your own home.*

3. *Never invite other parents out for an easy weekend meal.*

4. *Never talk about how sport should be part of the education curriculum.*

5. *Never mention that any red-blooded Australian man would not be seen dead with a glass of rosé in his hand.*

6. *Never mention that you don't understand how France can operate on a thirty-five hour week, a two-hour lunch break and seven weeks' paid annual holiday leave.*

7. *Never ask if the Marseille football team won the match the night before.*

8. *Never admit that you have French television but you never watch it because you prefer expensive English satellite television.*

To disobey these basic rules would make other parents look on in fright, like rabbits caught in the spotlight, laughing nervously at my Anglo-Saxon ways and my ignorance. On the rare occasions that a coffee was accepted, we would go to the local café in the village, where we consumed short black coffees while everyone else drew heavily on their umpteenth cigarette of the morning. Ten minutes later, coffees downed, cigarettes stubbed out, butts thrown out into the street or into a nearby dying pot plant, hands were shaken, or for those who had been friends since kindergarten there would be the Provençal three kisses to the cheek; more cigarettes were bought and everyone scattered back to their busy lives.

It was against this background that I had thrown caution to the wind and invited my French friends to bridge the cultural divide between the French and the mad Australians, who wanted to have an outdoor luncheon in the middle of winter. They were ready to learn about cricket, meat pies and beer. The Australian tradition is to bring a plate or a carton of beer or some wine to contribute to any festivities, but after long discussions with Raymond, I felt that this would be too culturally confronting. Their presence would be enough.

The children were far more interested in Pam's promise to whip up some lamingtons, which had to be explained as a wonderful light vanilla cake concoction with a cream filling, rolled in chocolate and desiccated coconut. She had also promised a pavlova. Mimi and Harry promised their best friend Raphaël that it was the dessert to die for: a meringue base topped with fruit and whipped cream. The children idolised Pam because not only did she always look unflappable, but she also cooked great food. I couldn't help but pass the snide comment that she had the worst behaved and the worst looking dog in the area. Pickles was a snappy little fox terrier that tended to attack and kill chickens in their coops, given half the chance. These words were uttered well before I found out that our dog Zorro would turn out to be the biggest mistake I had made in France. It had not taken very long to discover that Zorro was spoilt and undisciplined and there was no one to blame but myself. Claire continued to point out that dogs took after their masters and I could only reply that I was neither sleek nor black. With no proper fence around the property, Zorro's latest trick was to escape from our home on a regular basis and forage in the garbage bins throughout the village. His fluorescent red bandanna was meant to keep him safe from hunters' wayward shots; instead it clearly identified him as the dog of Madame Taylor.

The morning of our festivities was clear but extremely cold. I sighed with relief that we would be able to have the barbecue outdoors and the cricket match could take place without the threat of rain. Claire and Patrick had promised to bring around their ping-pong table, at which we could seat twenty guests with enough leg and arm room. In anticipation of its arrival, Raymond began to move all extraneous furniture from the main living area to the garage. Having a cricket match in the undulating backyard around worm-infested prune and rotting cherry trees did not constitute the real deal in his books. Much to my chagrin, he wondered out loud if he would be the only one who knew the rules of cricket — and moreover, if the guests would be able to put their wine glasses down in time to catch the ball. If Raymond couldn't be sitting on a boat in the middle of

Sydney Harbour, beer in hand while eating prawns, at least he hoped that it would be possible to watch the Australian Day festivities on television; he moaned and carried on like a juvenile. There were times when I wished that he would disappear straight down to the earth's molten core via one of the many deep holes that housed the control valves for our garden irrigation system, and never come back. Yet another thing on the list of things to do: the metal safety lids never had turned up. My children had memorised the location of the holes, but my biggest concern was that in the fading light, someone could break a leg.

'Raymond, there's over a hectare of land. You must be able to find somewhere to play a game of cricket.' He and Harry were dispatched with a can of spray paint that they proposed to spray on the grass to show where the wicket would be. There was no blood link between them but as I watched them walk off together, shoulders sloping, sinking under the pressure of the tremendously difficult task, I wondered if they resembled each other due to their sex or if Harry considered Raymond as a role model.

Beautiful old white linen tablecloths covered the whole of the massive ping-pong table without looking like second-hand sheets; yet again Claire had waved her magic wand and created a fabulous table setting. The room was bedecked in Australian flags; iconic photographs taken from old calendars were tacked up on the walls along with other Australian paraphernalia, making the room look like an exhibition from an Australian souvenir shop. Twenty chairs and stools were squeezed around the table; leftover Christmas crackers had been discreetly placed near the youngest members of the party. Words for the Australian and French national anthems had been printed so the guests could sing along with the CD that had been made especially for the occasion. The blue skies continued to make a mockery of the previous evening's weather forecast for heavy rain or snow in the north and, for us living in the belt between Avignon and Aix-en-Provence, a small chance of snow flurries. The weather report manages to raise a laugh with every nationality, no matter where you are in the world — it is notoriously wrong. No snow flurries could be seen on the horizon. The sky was crystal clear, devoid of anything that resembled a fluffy cloud. Nothing would hamper our celebrations.

Our French contingent arrived and discreetly peered around; beers in neoprene holders printed with football team colours, Australian flags and other similar symbols of dubious taste were handed out to the guests as soon as they entered the gates. They were designed to keep the drinks cool, but that seemed completely unnecessary as the first of the predicted snow flurries fell.

The Australian XI versus the French was a huge success when Catherine, one of the Two Ladies, discovered that she was the Mistress of Spin. The wine flowed and food continued to arrive from the kitchen all day long. A wonderful feeling of bonhomie reigned. Those who could keep up the pace watched as the lunch turned into an afternoon tea party then into an impromptu dinner party, ending at two o'clock in the morning with Deirdre challenging the spelling of Fair or Fare in the title of the national anthem. It was time for everyone to go home. The Two Ladies staggered down the path to their house on the neighbouring property. Claire and Patrick left Raphaël sleeping in Harry's room while they held hands and wove their way along the path through the neighbour's vines and across the cherry fields that would lead them eventually to their house. Luckily, the biting wind muffled Deirdre's renditions of bawdy pub songs and confidently worded interpretations of the French national anthem as she accompanied them halfway along the track to her home, glass in hand.

Problems continued to be added to my list of things to do, but occasionally a few fell off. The lack of a proper fence around the property had been a source of immense worry, as I had found human and animal footprints scattered across the back section of the garden. The first time hunters took aim and let out a volley of shots across our property, I realised that no matter the expense, I needed to have a fence around the hectare. Jack decided that his grandchildren needed protection and I gratefully accepted his offer of some financial help to resolve this matter. Once the new fence was in place, the wild boars and other beasts kept me awake at night as they charged towards old feeding grounds that had now been fenced off.

I was not sure whether my father's generosity would extend to building a high wall around the Monet pond. Drowning has always been my biggest fear. By the beginning of winter, Zorro was big enough to learn a new trick: stealing clothes and sheets from the triple clotheslines. He overstepped the mark when he stole them and dragged them through the lily pond that was fast freezing over — but not fast enough. Luckily I was on hand to watch in horror as he cracked the thick ice on the pond and plunged into the freezing murky water. Fully clothed and finally able to shake myself into action, I jumped in to save him. Ignoring my heroic feat, the children took Zorro to dry in front of the fire, more concerned about potential brain damage to the dog than any danger to my health.

The 2003 season was off to a shaky start as we were still feeling the repercussions of September 11, but inquiries were turning into some solid bookings that made the prospect of a forced sale of one if not two of the properties recede just a little. Throughout the winter I had been working on a low-budget advertising scheme, focussing mainly on Internet companies that offered good rates and that were already well placed in

the French holiday rental market. Running some
advertising in the print media did not generate nearly
enough inquiries to warrant another spate of
advertisements. I had spent a vast quantity of time in
front of the computer screen, becoming faster at typing
and more computer literate, but it was still an
unquestionable fact that searching on the Internet was
exhausting and time-consuming. I set up tables to
cross-reference various rates against the circulations for
magazines and newspapers in Scandinavia, Germany
and the Netherlands. These tourists from the sunless
north represented tried and tested markets, and they
returned year after year, blocking the roads leading
down to the south of France with their fast Mercedes
and camping cars. Even Raymond, whom I often called
Doubting Thomas under my breath, was amazed at my
dogged determination to gather information and
watched me with guarded admiration as I revealed the
various ways that I was attacking the problem· of
nurturing a clientele base for my properties.

Information and reference sheets that I had initially
clipped into folders had finally been written into a
weighty volume that was left in the houses for the
clients. All the trips, restaurants, markets and various
places of interest in the Luberon and surrounding areas
were given our own personal tick of approval or the big
thumbs down. After I finished writing the large
information folder, a small seed had been sown at the

back of my mind: all of my life I had wanted to write, but I had never found nor taken the time to indulge in it seriously. Like most of my ideas, it was pushed to the back until it resurfaced six months later, when I blurted out in front of friends that I intended to write a memoir and put down on paper — or on a floppy disk, to be more precise — all of the memories, funny ideas and opinions that had been floating around in my head for decades.

My initial foray into serious writing had to be delayed, though, as a disaster was about to crash on my doorstep. There was yet another large-scale calamity waiting to happen: a disease called Severe Acute Respiratory Syndrome — shortened to SARS. On 14 February a report hit the media that over 300 cases of a severe form of pneumonia in the Guongdong Province of China had resulted in five deaths. By 15 March the World Health Organization issued a heightened global health alert as more cases of the mysterious illness had been found in Singapore and in Canada. That is when the bookings all but dried up. Few brave tourists from the southern hemisphere were prepared to pass through Singapore; those who did not need to travel did not and those with children decided that overseas travel was not high on their list of priorities.

Any precious time that had been set aside as writing time was consumed in a desperate search for Internet agencies that would list French properties on a free trial period. Little by little, it began to pay off. For some reason Canadians decided that it was time to pay a visit to the south of France — and better still, it was time to come to my properties.

CHAPTER THIRTEEN

Provençal Painting Lesson

My short time in business had shown me that there was no room for compromise when it came to financial decisions. Looking at my 2003 booking sheets, I could scrape by, and in theory I would still be in business at the end of the year, but the letters telling me yet again to sell one of the properties were ten feet high — downsize as soon as possible, they read. It was exhausting trying to budget for the monthly mortgage payments. Even if we had a dramatic turnaround, with clients booking every property for every week in 2003, the truth was that I was overextended and therefore had become financially vulnerable.

Launching a small business in a field in which I had no knowledge and little to no experience (except in basic housekeeping), there had been a steep learning curve with hard lessons learnt along the way. Any little crumbs of information were ferreted away for use at a later date; knowledge was gleaned from as many sources as possible. My acquaintances in the English-speaking group had rental properties and gave advice freely and generously, without fear of competition, as everyone had something slightly different to offer holiday-makers. Small properties within the village with no parking did not compete with those that were far from the village with large sparkling pools, well-kept gardens and parking at the door. We all had a common link: the problems always remained the same — perpetual leaks, broken dishwashers or washing machines plagued everyone. I had developed a close and happy relationship with the plumbers, electricians and washing machine repairmen in Apt. As soon as they heard my accent on the telephone on a Saturday, they would know that I had yet another urgent job for them.

Refurbishments and repairs were a necessary evil of the business; they were time-consuming, costly and left the owners feeling pathetic and inadequate, asking themselves why they did not have the necessary skills to fix some niggling problem themselves. Unless they were urgent and interfered with the running of the property, small problems went onto an expanding list for winter, when the necessary time would be found for some basic do-it-yourself repairs and tradesmen were slightly more available.

By mid-March we were still in the throes of winter, with no sign of a thaw. Understandably, the children were not particularly interested in giving me advice about what to do with our future, so Claire was now becoming my business confidante. We could decide whether to sell Place de la Fontaine at a later date; meanwhile, it was time to spruce up the property that we had called home for twenty weeks during 2000.

Claire looked at me in total horror when I told her that I intended to paint the entire house by myself — there was no one else, after all. She felt that paintbrushes should be added to the long list — along with screwdrivers, electrical drills and any kitchen appliance with sharp moving parts — of devices I was banned from operating. I was notorious for breaking, jamming and snapping appliances — I could destroy any toy and computer that was not 100 per cent idiot proof. In my defence I would bleat pathetically that I was a time-poor mother who did not have a mechanical type of mind. Since I waltzed around the house until ten o'clock in my mauve kimono dressing gown, teacup in one hand and newspaper in the other, Claire muttered under her breath that she thought that I was perhaps just bone lazy and didn't want to learn. She, on the other hand, worked like the Roadrunner on amphetamines. I scrambled in her wake, trying to keep up with her speed and efficiency.

Our differences aside, she was first and foremost a Frenchwoman, and from earlier experience I thought that it was best to ask her opinion about paint as I would never hear the end of it if her views had not been aired, analysed, discussed and then finally accepted. Compromise came into our relationship a lot: she told me what was best and I had to agree. When it came to paint, fabric choices, colours, clothes, cars, wood suppliers and repairmen, I allowed her to rule me with an iron fist. Somehow we managed never to fight, and remained best friends who saw each other nearly every day, and when the final decision was taken we were both happy with the direction we were taking.

Place de la Fontaine had last been painted from top to bottom a little over three years ago, before it was used for short-term holiday rentals. After only two years of fairly constant traffic, the property was looking tired and in desperate need of some new paint. I could never understand how a house could look so weary and worn in such a relatively short period of time. I had never before had the need to paint a house every two years. It was Claire who pointed out the obvious: every week, clients arrived with heavy suitcases that they dragged rather than lifted, scraping the steps with their heavy loads, bumping into the walls looking for light switches. I maintained that the majority of my clients were vain and lazy like me and probably just needed glasses and stronger arms.

It was time for a visit to my friend Kamila's *chambre d'hôte* at the top of the main road in our village. She and her husband Pierre had created the most spectacular guesthouse, which was also an art gallery and a residence for artists from all across the world. You were guaranteed to meet interesting people actively involved in projects that were fascinating, especially compared to my very mundane life of washing and ironing sheets. Their house was large and rambling, built across several levels. On each floor corridors led off to bedrooms, bathrooms, the art workshop and, of course, the walled garden that contained secrets and magic, which was reached from the house by a wooden drawbridge. Every room in the house featured a colour theme, painted in *chaux* — a kind of chalk mixed with ochres from the region. Claire and I went through the house admiring the effect that Kamila had been able to achieve with the kind of bold colours that you would normally avoid: lurid purples, deep chocolates, violent hot pinks and almost fluorescent greens. Although it was fascinating to see the bold colours in action at Kamila's enormous house with its huge rooms and high ceilings, Claire and I agreed that Place de la Fontaine needed very creamy light colours.

Kamila was an expert at making *chaux*: take a clean cement mixer, fill it with white chalky *chaux*, add large quantities of ochre pigments of your choice and enough water to make a thick paste, then switch on the cement mixer until there are no lumps or bubbles of pigment. Simple. Just like making a cake.

Down to Apt we went to visit Chavin, a leading ochre specialist in the Luberon. In this Aladdin's cave of colours Claire and I made our choices, after great deliberation and assistance from the staff. All the correct wide, thick brushes were bought and more advice was taken. Apparently we could not go wrong. There would be no sickening fumes, no mess and no gloss to paint around the wooden window frames. What I didn't know was that it would be like painting with thick glue. After the kitchen had been painted, Claire came to inspect my handiwork and even she was impressed with how difficult it was to apply the thick paint, and my improving biceps. As I moved from room to room, I became more adept at slapping on the paint in large sweeping brush strokes using a herringbone pattern, giving a slightly uneven rustic look that went perfectly with the crooked walls, nooks and crannies.

Kamila arrived one day to inspect the choice of colours and snorted in ridicule when she saw that the same colour had been employed throughout. She had also come to invite me to dinner. Kamila was an outstanding cook and a consummate hostess. Her Polish background and her journeys across Europe gave her an ability to cook many different types of food and speak passably in English, German, several Eastern European dialects and of course flawless but heavily accented French.

That evening as we all gathered in her exotic salon, she spoke in English to make her Anglophone guests more at ease, announcing to the group: 'Yes, look everybody, come outside. I have a beautiful shining new vulva.'

Her command of the French language was perfect, but the same could not be said when it came to English. I heard someone murmur, 'I think she means Volvo, dear.'

Expensive perfumes hung in the air and everywhere I looked there were dandies in their finery: men with smart linen suits, waistcoats in jacquard prints, linen shirts with ruffles and flounces. Exquisite scraps of beautiful fabrics adorned the women's reed-thin bodies, exposing large areas of their equally beautiful buffed skin. As usual, their undergarments were taking pride of place as necklines plunged to the waist and minuscule portions of lace and silk covered their modesty. Barely. Through the throngs of guests, I spied a man who was apparently charming the pants off a harem of ladies around him. Their girlish laughter and frenetic batting of eyelashes were positively nauseating. Whether or not this man was on the lookout for a new mistress or wife, the word was that he was one of France's largest private industrialists and the women were doing their best to be first in the queue or at least be noticed. They were swarming around him like the proverbial bees around the honey pot. I could see that he was waiting for me to join the queue so I deliberately turned on my heels and headed off in the opposite direction. He moved towards me, held out his hand and caught me; in rapid French he addressed me: '*Bonsoir*, my name is Jungpo. It would give me great pleasure if you sat next to me this evening for dinner.'

With his guttural Provençal accent, I managed to understand one word in five spoken to me during the course of the evening. He told me something about the Eiffel Tower and how his company had recently installed some new electrical fitting on it, which made me assume that Jungpo was some sort of electrician. I had been mildly terrified when he insisted on using the intimate '*tu*' form instead of the very polite '*vous*' form for 'you'. It was far too familiar for my liking so I stuck with '*monsieur*' and '*vous*' and left his company and dinner as soon as possible. I discovered many months later that his name was not Jungpo, which did not sound particularly French to me, but Jean-Paul, which did. I also learnt that he was not an electrician. It was a long time before I met him again.

~~

The children breathed a sigh of relief that the painting was taking place somewhere other than where they lived, and was not interrupting their schedules, which consisted mainly of hours of homework, television watching and sitting at the table with their mouths open waiting to be fed yet again. Although I had risen slightly in their estimation during the past year with my capacity for hard work and early morning starts and the amount of washing and ironing I did, they did not want their friends to see me in my painting clothes, which consisted of track pants and several layers of very ugly clothing, most of them Raymond's rejected winter clothes. Through Claire, I learnt later, much too late, that a Frenchwoman would dress in her good clothes, take a bag of painting or exercise clothes and then change in a discreet spot. When seen in public a Frenchwoman represents her family to the world and on no account would she consider letting her standards drop. Paint-bespattered clothes or Lycra exercise pants should only be worn indoors, well away from view. The biggest, and perhaps the only, exception is bike pants: they are acceptable on men and women on Sundays for a bike ride. Needless to say, good lacy underwear and tiny knickers should be worn at all times. Standing in the paint aisle in the handyman shop, I realised that I would have to put more effort into my appearance; according to the children I was a sartorial train wreck. My standards had slipped to rock bottom.

Like most parents, negotiation was the basis of my relationship with the children. As they wandered down the track towards the bus stop in the early morning winter fog one day, laden down with schoolbooks and encased in their padded overcoats, I smiled to think how my babies had grown up so fast and now resembled small black bears, albeit with backpacks, trundling down the lane. Sentiment turned to alarm as a volley of shots rang across the path from the hunters who, in the mist, thought that my children were prey. Mimi and Harry could not bring themselves to wear fluorescent vests with flashing lights, so the bargain was struck that I would drive them to the end of the lane and wait with them for the school bus, ducked down low so their friends on the bus wouldn't see that their mother was wearing her pyjamas underneath her overcoat — or worse still, my Australian green and gold painting balaclava.

Even with an early start in the morning and the children staying at school at lunchtime, the painting in Place de la Fontaine was taking a lot longer than I initially thought. As I went up into the room on the top floor, I realised that the long ladders would be necessary. When I had been a small child, my sister Kate and I would watch in wonderment as our father hung suspended from the roof high above the ground or off the veranda. It must be in the genes: neither of us has any fear. I also had no money to hire someone else to do this task. I was confident that I was up to it. Claire was confident that I would fall. She had insisted on being on site on the ground floor, where she was making new slipcovers for the two sofas. She felt that the day I fell from the long ladder, she should be there to pick up the pieces. Until now, she had always been right.

High up above the stairwell in the far corner, deep in thought, I tried to extend my hand too far, overbalanced and off I came. This house, and in particular this room, had been extremely lucky for me before; once again, my luck stayed with me as I fell, bouncing down the ladder and then onto the hard floor. The extra layers of clothes and my extra winter weight protected me from any major injuries, but not from Claire's ire. 'Just concentrate on the painting. Don't think about anything else. It is a wonder that you weren't seriously hurt.'

'Claire, that's the problem. I am painting this house because I know that I have to sell it. I have to sell this property as soon as possible but the biggest problem is that I don't want to. Look at this place; it has never looked as pretty. By the way, I've made another decision. That wall I have just finished has to be repainted a dirty blue. What do you think?'

From my perspective, lying on the ground, it was evident that the long wall needed some sort of colour. I hoped that the agonising decision to sell or not would be just as easy, but it took many months to arrive at the final solution.

~~~

Painting is very cleansing for the mind, like ironing sheets: an expanse of a neutral colour and the end product looks fantastic. My mind had been spring-cleaned and I was clear about our next move: a quick Easter trip to Sydney before the 2003 season started. We had enough frequent flyer points to redeem them for one adult ticket for Mimi, and as Harry was still flying as a child the total amount would not be too horrendous. The biggest expense was hiring a car, and even that looked economical compared with European prices. It would be a whirlwind trip. The children usually stayed with their aunts and uncles and I stayed with Raymond, but this time we would not be seeing Raymond; he would be on a family visit to New Zealand, he said. Our Big Discussion was delayed yet again and I caught myself too many times being grateful for his absence. Our family home in Mosman was being rented out. I walked past the ill-kept garden and noted the general chaos that appeared to reign in the house with a certain amount of detachment, as it now only represented for me some bricks and mortar; a good investment but no longer our home. Some friends were away for Easter; others were busy with their holidays. The strong ties to Sydney appeared to be loosening.

I had met up with a university friend who was now a highly respected journalist. Susan had listened to my story and had encouraged me not to be afraid to write. I felt as though my brain was ready to explode with sentences and words that had been floating through my grey matter for the past decade. I had made up my mind to work seriously on a memoir after our return to France. I had no idea how long it would take or — more to the point — if I had the necessary literary and computer skills. Too many people had novels sitting in the bottom drawer incomplete and unpublished. Did I really want to go down that path? I knew by the end of our very short stay that my fingers were itching to get to a keyboard and make sense of my rough thoughts and jottings.

~~

At home in France again, the children slipped back into their school routine, happy in the knowledge of what May would bring them: more holidays. In France, three out of four weeks in May have public holidays and sometimes the unions even add an extra day to make it a long weekend for the workers. May always makes me shudder with disbelief. And school children cheer if the holidays fall on a Tuesday; it means that their weekend extends from Saturday through to Thursday, as Wednesday is a day off.

Harry, like Mimi, needed some extra coaching to help him with his language skills, to prepare him for his eventual entrance into high school. I found it difficult to explain to a ten-year-old the need to learn lists of verbs and tenses: the subjunctive and the past historic

tenses made his eyes water. These were areas I had dealt
with when I was at university, but it was mandatory for
primary school children to have a working knowledge
of these lists that unfortunately just had to be learnt off
my heart.

I continued to maintain that it was necessary for
both of them to speak to me in English, and to speak in
French only when there were non-English speakers
with us. Our family council had voted that we would
stay until the end of their schooling here in France, so it
was important that there was some balance in their
lives. They read and spoke in English but rarely wrote
emails or postcards in English. Astérix comic books and
French magazines aimed at the pre-adolescent market
were consumed with pleasure and gusto as they became
more and more French.

As in most education systems, support classes for those
who needed help in specialised skills were fairly thin on
the ground and infrequent. The local village school had
no access to help. The director of the school, Monsieur
Champeau, had investigated various avenues and came up
with two half-hour classes in Apt. This had been
wonderful as a beginning to their learning, but Harry had
advanced to a point where he needed some quite specific
help. Anne George's name was put forward by one of the
secretaries from the high school. Formerly a teacher who
taught children in their last year of primary school, after a
family tragedy she had taken early retirement and now

offered coaching to a select few. My fingers were crossed
that she would have the time and the inclination to rise
to the challenge of teaching Harry verbs, tenses,
vocabulary, mathematics, geography, history and generally
inspiring him into high school. In short, she would have
to teach him all over again from scratch.

~~

The 2003 season started off slowly, but little by little
bookings were made — and most owners in the rental
accommodation business breathed a small sigh of relief.
Except for Deirdre, who was struggling with coming to
terms with the finality of death and all of the problems
that seemed to go hand in hand with it. Her husband
Geoffrey had lost his battle with throat cancer and
finally passed away, leaving Deirdre with a mountain of
medical bills and complex problems with taxes and
Geoff's will. These problems were compounded daily.
Although she was a great tap-dancer, she was very
shaky in her knowledge of French and how to deal
with the banking system, lawyers and officials from the
mayor's office.

My mother had died shortly after my husband. After
their funerals I decided never to attend another one.
No friendly words of support or love were forthcoming
from me when my best friend and tennis partner of five
years buried her father and mother within the same

year; I couldn't trust my emotions at any funeral ever
again. There are some times you just have to stand on
the sidelines. But when Geoff died, Deirdre held a huge
wake at their home to thank her friends for their years
of support during his illness and to celebrate the
generosity and warmth of this man among family and
friends. All the expatriate community, the mayor's office
from Roussillon, and some of Geoff's nurses and
doctors attended. Amongst the safety of the pots and
pans in the kitchen I thought I could just ease into the
background of the gathering. The churning of my
stomach made me think otherwise, prompting a quick
exit to throw up violently in the garden.

Like most new widows, Deirdre was brilliant and
appearing to cope when she was in a crowd. However,
it was when she was on her own that the rot set in and
she would call me. We attacked the financial problems
first; the emotional ones had to be left until much later.
I translated accounts and threatening letters that were
arriving, making pages of lists of things that she had to
do in order for me to help her. Strategies and meetings
were marked down, columns of figures of income and
expenditures were written down, added up and
totalled; she was haemorrhaging financially. We walked
around the problems and looked from all the angles, but
in the end the only sensible option was to sell
everything, pay off the debts and start with a clean
page.

In the still of early evening I sat in the dusk, teacup in hand, mulling over the problems that beset Deirdre's life and thinking how it was in a process of flux and change. Chaos was ruling but at the same time there seemed to be some sort of advancement. Was that chaos theory? I made a note to look it up on the Internet and read more about it. There were so many parallels in life. We all take such different paths that lead to the same destination: love, loss, joy, heartache — then eventually we find out that we are all merely mortals, on this earth for such a short time.

CHAPTER FOURTEEN

The Poisoned
Right Arm

My favourite month, May, brought the gypsies into the district to prepare for the cherry harvest in June. The locals despised them as a necessary evil: but they worked hard, when the conditions were hot and the hours long. The cherry harvest could not wait while the French took their two-hour lunch break and the extra days that linked the weekend to the public holidays in May. Night after night I could hear beautiful melodies from a guitar floating across the vineyards and distant cherry orchards. One night after listening to the same haunting tunes, my curiosity was piqued by the music carried in the stillness of the night. The gypsies had set up camp in the only large opening accessible for their large vehicles and caravans. I was like a moth to their flame and within moments I was out our front gate, walking through the fields towards them.

From a vantage spot just metres from their fires I watched as one handsome swarthy young man clutched his guitar between his legs and caressed the instrument, running his fingers gently up and down the neck of the guitar while the outlines of people around him sang in tune to his song — which, even though the language was incomprehensible to my ears, I could tell was about life and sorrow. No matter our colour or race, we are, after all, just the same.

The gypsies were like a plague of locusts that arrived in large white vans filled to the brim with brown-faced children; after three weeks the cherry trees were stripped bare, and the vans and caravans were gone. Lines once full of colourful clothing strung up between the cherry trees surrounding the camps were empty; the sheets no longer flapped in the stiff breeze. The campsite became barren overnight. Everything had been tidied up and swept away; the gypsies had disappeared like the proverbial puff of smoke, their romantic life on the road leading them to their next destination.

Another gypsy entered my life: my father Jack, accompanied by his new girlfriend, Cecily, whom I had never met. Across a crowded room in the summer of 1953, Jack had spied Cecily. Their eyes met and fireworks went off. Jack was twenty-six and head over heels in love with Cecily. He was still living in his home town of Glasgow but decided that taking a young bride of twenty to the shores of Australia was too much to ask. Cecily went on to marry his best friend, Les. Fifty years later, after my mother and Les had both died, Jack and Cecily took up exactly where they left off. Cecily continued to live in Scotland and Jack in Mosman, but they were meeting up to spend the summer in France with each other and with me.

I was nervous about accepting someone into my home as my father's new girlfriend, since my parents had had a long, passionate love affair and I couldn't imagine Jack with anyone else. But I found that this awkward moment lasted no more than two seconds, which was all the time it took for me to realise that Cecily was charming, open and funny. She too had had a long and loving marriage. It seemed very normal that they should be together. I soon decided that Cecily was an unexpected bonus in my father's life, and she was quickly drawn into the family circle.

Both she and Jack were in tremendous form and extremely high spirits. She was teaching him the rudiments of bridge but they told jokes and entertained the children as a necessary diversion from the intense concentration that was needed. Laughter and gaiety reigned in our house as the old jokes were trotted out and my children fell about holding their sides just as Kate and I had when we were young. Only on extremely rare occasions does Jack allow his serious side to surface. He should have been a Zen Buddhist or a

Rastafarian; he has always been very cool and relaxed about any problems in life. Incredible for someone who started life in the Jewish slums of Glasgow.

Their mirth and high spirits were much needed, but sometimes I also needed some peace and quiet to do my accounts away from the prying eyes of my father. Jack wanted to pick cherries and Cecily wanted to make jam. Claire's next-door neighbour, Roland, owned the vast tracts of cherry fields that surrounded Claire's little rented cottage. I resorted to the bush telegraph system and asked Claire to ask him if extra hands could be employed to help with the harvest of the Big Blacks, and if payment could be made in cherries.

The cherry fields had belonged to Roland's family for decades. His father had farmed these fields and now, as Roland neared his fiftieth birthday, it was he who was in sole control. He gave the impression that he was the type of farmer who would prefer to be sitting in the shadows of a haystack, a shaft of wheat in his mouth, dozing in the midday sun ruminating about the philosophy of life.

The family's land spread across the sunny slopes of St Saturnin les Apt; like all of the region's farmers, they also had large tracts of land in other areas so that if and when the hail ruined the crops in one area, the devastation would not be complete. Roland spent all of his year looking after his trees so that once a year the crop could be harvested and the cycle would recommence. The fields were divided up into the different varieties of cherries. The white cherries were taken to the enormous fruit factory in Apt, where they were turned into glacé fruit for confectionery. The reds were sent to large markets all across Europe, ready for jam making or table presentation. The last fields to be picked were the enormous Grosses Rouges (Big Reds), far too good to turn into jam, but outstanding for table presentation. These were the Rolls Royce of cherries.

Gentle words had come back from Roland via Claire that it was a business he was running, not a seniors' holiday camp. There was no problem if Jack would like to pick a small bucket of cherries for himself, but not the cherries needed for the trays at the market; there was a certain amount of skill needed and unfortunately there was no time to explain how to pick and sort.

Some people from the village and the neighbouring areas were employed as seasonal workers to finish off the harvest. Many mothers worked in the fields as it gave families the opportunity to supplement the funds needed to go on their annual August holiday. Our neighbours, the Two Ladies, were in the fields, as were Claire's older children, who from the age of seventeen had worked as often and as long as possible in order to increase their paltry living allowance and help pay for their studies in Grenoble.

Even Patrick and Claire were employed in the cherry fields. Although Patrick was a self-employed electrician, he was an integral part of the team during the weeks when the carpet system was in operation. This method could only be used in certain fields, ones where robust trees were appropriately spaced in large, wide alleys. He drove the tractor that pulled a metal rod over six metres in length on which there was a roll of green closely woven plastic fabric. The long rod was laid out beside each tree: a slit in the fabric allowed the carpet to be laid around the tree, covering a large area on the ground. A thick heavily padded collar was wrapped around the tree and then attached to the machinery, pulling it taut. The vibrations from the machinery caused the cherries to fall gently to the ground. The carpet was then rolled up onto the rod, spilling the cherries into a trough where the young workers stood, verifying that there were no marks or imperfections on the produce. The cherries were packed into plastic crates and then onto a forklift truck that took the crates to the cold room behind the farmhouse. In the coolness of early evening Claire would spend hours grading the cherries into the correct wooden crates lined with fancy paper, fruit down, stems up — all pointing the same way. Every day during the harvest, in the pitch dark well before sunrise, the truck was loaded and driven to the fruit and vegetable wholesale markets in Châteaurenard, on the southeastern fringes of Avignon — a good forty minutes away. By six o'clock, Roland's crates of perfect cherries would be ready for auction at the markets and he would be free to join the other farmers in conversation over a steaming cup of coffee and a freshly baked croissant.

Early in the harvest I had worked in the cherry field for an insignificant two hours — perhaps not even as much as that. Nothing was going to get in the way of the celluloid images I had of myself, starring in a Provençal landscape, floating through the cherry trees laden with bright red globes dressed in a light cotton dress, apron and a pretty scarf knotted around my hair, swinging my woven straw basket. The harsh reality hit home as the midday sun climbed high in the sky; the clock hands seemed to freeze in time as the furnace-like heat became completely unbearable. Mouthfuls of bruised and non-marketable cherries and the incessant noise of the tractors served only to make me feel ill and incapable of work. Roland had rolled his eyes skyward when he saw my pathetic harvest of cherries and banished me to the trees in the distance, where he did not have to be infuriated by my ineptitude and I could go about my fantasy in private without harm to his product.

~~

Emails to the Latin Lover were becoming increasingly spasmodic, short and even curt. The huge distance between us was widening. We both struggled under the constraints of maintaining a relationship where distance and time were major components. As always, my sister Kate nailed it on the head: 'You're a masochist. Wake up to yourself. What do you think, that he is waiting for you patiently to come home to Sydney to his little love nest that you visit every couple of months? Don't you get it? Raymond is wonderful and caring, but he just doesn't love you enough. Get over him. Move on. Turn the page. How much clearer do you want me to spell it out? You live in different countries, even in different hemispheres. How on earth do you expect it to work?'

Only after hours of reflection about how much we really loved each other did it dawn on me that I, too, loved Raymond a lot less these last few years. I had left Sydney with little idea of how to steer my family's future as a single parent; now, three years down the track, I had built up a business and started to put down roots in a foreign land. The children were happy, extremely well liked and growing like weeds. Whatever my failings, I had to be doing something right — with or without a man by my side. I had faced the fact that I would prefer to have a solitary life rather than be shackled to someone with whom I did not, quite frankly, share a common goal. When it came to the future, Raymond and I were not even looking in the same direction.

Raymond was on his way to visit us for his mid-term break in July and I had promised myself that during this holiday we would have a proper adult discussion about commitment and love. A boots and all, out in the open type of discussion to clear the air. My heart was yearning for true love, but as always my head was screaming that everyone was right: I was flogging a dead horse. Raymond regarded us as lifelong friends who happened to have a great sex life together. I wanted something more than that. Something had to give and that something would be him. I needed a concrete expression of his commitment in some form or another. Enrolment in a Latin course in an English university that was close to an airport so that he could visit regularly, with the cheap fares between England and France, would be more than acceptable. Having children to educate, a business in France and a particularly difficult temperament, I was not prepared to compromise my position one iota.

Now that I had that clearly in my mind, I tried to think of the best time and place to have the Big Discussion. Obviously it wouldn't be at Sarah's 50th birthday party, which was to be held the evening Raymond was due to arrive. Sarah, a member of the local English-speaking community, was the epitome of a modern Englishwoman. Jane Austen might have had a great deal of influence on her forebears, but Sarah was too busy to be caught whimpering or simpering about life over cups of tea in the garden. She never displayed any known vices in public: no rude words passed her lips, there was no excessive eating or drinking and no smoking. On a regular basis she exercised her labradors, Fat Freddie and Lazy Daisy, partly for their own good and partly for her own. She constantly watched her weight and adamantly stuck to diets — one to prepare for summer and then one for winter. She had only been married once, had three perfectly acceptable good-looking nearly adult children and the two sweet-natured labradors. In short, she and I had absolutely nothing in common except for the dogs but I, like all of her acquaintances, held Sarah in high regard.

Since her real birthday in May, plans for the big party had been in constant revision. At long last the mid-July date had arrived, and the weather was going to be perfect. The marquee had been erected beside the pool, the dance floor installed. The lawn had been mowed into a green carpet, lights dangled in the trees, and candles were ready to be lit and flicker romantically along the dry stone walls.

Raymond had had the trip from hell to wing his way to us in France: a delay of several hours in Singapore followed by an unscheduled emergency stop in Frankfurt, followed by a further delay in Marseille. By the time he arrived, thirty hours after leaving Sydney, he could barely talk or stand upright, due to severe jet lag, tiredness and drunkenness. This time it was he who was coming for a quick Winter Escape of seventeen days; already he felt as though most of them had been spent on the plane. It was out of the question to take him to Cavaillon to hire a bow tie and black suit for the James Bond theme party. He wanted to sleep for twenty-four hours, not sit in a poorly fitting penguin suit. Leaving him snoring in bed at home while I went as a single guest was becoming an increasingly attractive idea. The writing was on the wall: our relationship was Doomed to Destruction. Unfortunately, after a short nap, Raymond decided to accompany me to the party, which turned out to be hideous mistake. Already drunk and disorderly, he rapidly became out of control; mistaking a young brunette for me, he declared his amorous intentions before passing out cold at the table.

Once again, I found myself out of step with Mother Nature and love. July was truly one of the most jaw-dropping times in the Luberon. There is the heat of summer, with cicadas singing, heralding the beauty that is about to unfold: the swollen heads of lavender bursting into colour, the patchwork of bleached fields of shorn wheat alongside those that still ripple with washed-out yellow wheat waiting for harvest, the oversized sunflowers and the grapevines groaning under the weight of abundant leaves and the beginnings of purple grapes. It is in July that suddenly the clear summer light turns the

Luberon hills a deep shade of purple at sunset. The light reverts back to a wonderful glow after the heat of a summer's day.

In the midst of all this beauty, work went on. While I put on loads of sheets to wash, Claire sat at her machine sewing her latest set of creamy linen armchair covers. We spent more and more time working together, and the conversation flowed as she told me more and more about her marriage at eighteen and divorce at thirty. Her formative years were spent in wealth and privilege but that changed when her parents separated and her mother followed her heart by running off with her true love. Claire's mother's family disapproved so strongly that all contact with her was severed. Hard times and disaster followed when Claire's stepfather, Mr True Love, walked out the door into the arms of another. History repeated itself when Claire was seventeen: she went from dux of her year to dunce when she, too, followed her heart, dropped out of school and married her True Love. Claire came to bitterly regret turning her back on her education, and as a result was now passionate about schooling. Her children — and now mine by association — had to excel in every test, every exam and every project. Education was everything. She set a punishing workload and expected everyone to keep pace with her. Her mind was quick, analytical and clever — that made her the perfect associate in my burgeoning business.

Sometimes I wondered why I continued with a business that was only just limping along, teetering on the verge of bankruptcy and giving me more grief than financial gain. There was no end to the toil. Fluffy white towels would come to the laundry sometimes covered in boot polish — or in one case grass stains, where a client had cleaned his golf clubs. Clients continued to call about washing machines that did not work when they weren't even plugged in.

'Don't forget I have to deal with the huge amount of garbage that clients leave behind. Remember that time when the clients left bags of week-old dirty nappies in the garage and mashed banana all over the cushions?' Claire's eyes crinkled up with laughter.

'Well, what about the nasty stuff I find under the beds!' I was not going to be outdone by Claire. Working in such close contact with the evidence of people's hygiene, it was sometimes very difficult to maintain a sense of humour. But after we swapped some of the worst horror stories, Claire pointed out we had been really blessed in the most part with fantastic clients who loved and truly appreciated the properties, often bursting into tears when they arrived and saw the bunch of roses and bottle of wine that greeted them. I was a little out of sorts, Claire suggested, and on the whole the season was progressing quite well and there had been no major hiccups.

After we had run through the list of things to do by

the end of the week for the new clients, Claire turned her attention to things closer to home. She could no longer stand by watching me eat myself up with indecision and confusion. I was red-eyed from silently sobbing into the incessant piles of ironing as I tried to sort out my emotional life. Raymond needed to be extricated from my life just as Place de la Fontaine needed to be sold. The solution to my problems was evident, she said. Over the bales of washing, she told me the story of the Poisoned Right Arm; a story that I was sure she had made up, though she said it was a tale passed down in Provençal folklore. A snake bit a woman one day in the forest. There was no medical assistance and the woman struggled as best she could, tying her right arm up in a tourniquet and pressure bandages. As time went by the wound would heal and then suddenly pus would ooze out and the wound would open again. It was no good. The arm was slowly poisoning her whole body. She has to take the decision to either die with the arm or save herself by cutting off the arm. She oscillates between the choices, confused and cross at her indecisiveness. One morning she wakes up and she knows that it is time to cut the arm off. The woman cuts off her arm, recovers, and learns with great surprise that her left arm is very strong and that her life is different but healthier without the other arm. At night she often feels as though her right arm is still there, but after time that absence is barely felt.

My love and admiration for Claire was immense, but I couldn't listen to her anecdotes about poison and love. She was of the opinion that it took at least two full years for the poison to work itself through after the loss of something that had been akin to a marriage. Tears were now coursing down my cheeks: 'Don't meddle in my affairs, Claire. I do not have a poisoned arm. I have Raymond and I will amputate him when I am good and ready. Let me tell you that it will be this week, not in two years' time!'

Whether or not this is what Claire had intended, I was now determined to end my relationship with Raymond as soon as possible. Maybe I had enough poison in my system? Maybe it was just time? My temper tantrums, black moods and general meanness gave Raymond an idea that all was not well with me and that something nasty was brewing. Most of his time was spent in the company of the children or with Kit, drinking large quantities of beer while watching sport at the bar down in Apt. His holiday was coming to an end and as yet nothing special had been arranged for the children's long summer holiday in August. A quick and inexpensive trip to Paris seemed to fit the bill. Before Raymond's departure we could spend a couple of days seeing the sights, something that everyone would enjoy.

Paris in summer is traditionally said to be stifling hot, airless and unpleasant. It is empty of all Parisians,

who have packed their cars and driven down to
Provence or the Côte d'Azur, leaving only the tourists
wandering around in the vain hope of finding some
shade under the large leafy plane trees that line the
boulevards or luxuriating in a short reprieve in the
coolness of the large halls in the Louvre or the Musée
d'Orsay. That is August — but sometimes you can be
lucky and get a few days of bearable weather, which is
what we had. We walked from one monument to
another, across the streets of Paris, back and forth across
the Seine, zigzagging our way past the lost tourists
clutching maps in their sweaty hands, finding places of
interest and out of the way galleries that had a famous
painting or sculpture which called for an hour's visit to
enrich our cultural experience.

Lying in our hotel bed afterwards with my arms and
legs wrapped around my Latin Lover, I opened my
heart and said what had to be said. It was time to say
goodbye. I did not want him to come back to us in
France. We would not be visiting him in Sydney.
Finally, our relationship was over. Over meant over.
Completely finished. The Big Discussion that I had
been prevaricating over for so long was now out in the
open and the words had been said. A tremendous peace
and calm descended on me and I had the most
wonderful spiritual feeling of contentment and
happiness. It was over. We could remain friends, but no
longer lovers. Our lives would no longer be entwined.

A snore rose up from the sheets. 'Did you hear anything I just said? Don't you dare tell me that you are sleeping!' A hand came up and Raymond dragged me into the crook of his arm. 'Yes. As usual you are right. We will talk about this tomorrow. You've had far too much to drink.'

~~

At three o'clock in the morning, when my liver was struggling to process an excess of alcohol, I woke drenched in sweat. Lights were flashing. 'Warning! Warning, Will Robinson!' the robot in *Lost in Space* used to say while thrashing his arms about. I continued to thrash in the sheets. During our first years in France I used to sing lines from songs about staying or leaving. Tomorrow at the airport I would kiss Raymond deeply and wave him goodbye. Misty images of the last scenes between Ingrid Bergman and Humphrey Bogart in *Casablanca* came flooding through my mind. Now that it was decided, all I needed was sleep. My mother's words played on a continuous loop in my head: wise sayings about leading horses to water but you can't make them drink and other jolly proverbs that only seemed to concern the animal kingdom. I had tried and failed to make Raymond love me; now it was time for both of us to move on.

Red lights flashed before my lightly closed eyes.

Epilepsy. I was having an epileptic fit. My brain had blown a fuse over my emotional and romantic notions about life; even my brain had given up on me. I sat up with a start: 'Raymond, wake up. I think I'm dying. Lights are flashing in my head. I can't go on like this any more. Why don't you love me?' My words were muffled as he threw me back onto the pillows.

'Do be quiet. You had too much wine at dinner. I know exactly what you need.' He went off to the bathroom to fetch me a glass of water. 'You are a complete nut case. You are not having a fit. It is just those horrific lights flashing on the Eiffel Tower. Can you believe that some moron has put flashing lights all up and down one of the world's greatest monuments? How can the French abuse their national treasures like that? Here, drink this.' Raymond had very strong views about the Disneyfication — a word he invented — of art and architecture. He hated the way lights were strung up to highlight famous buildings and art galleries put shows together just for popular appeal. I ignored the beginnings of his diatribe about the demise of culture in the Western world as he nuzzled my neck and my breasts. 'I don't know what you are going on about. I love you and I love the children. I would walk over glass to get to you if you were in trouble. Nothing would keep me from your side. I've known you for two decades. I am not giving you up. We are not breaking up. How many times do I have to tell you that you are the only woman on this earth for me? I love you and I adore you. Let's do something really special in Italy, if that is what you really want. We can go to Venice with the kids for Christmas or their February holidays. Would that suit you? Now either shut up and get some sleep or I will do something extremely rude to you. Take your pick.'

As my Latin Lover took me back in his arms and commenced the horizontal samba I knew that what we had was True Love, even though there was a minuscule voice in the back of my head telling me not to be seduced but to stick with my decision. The words he uttered were not a proposal. He had fobbed me off yet again. Raymond did not want an Italian wedding. He just wanted me to go back to sleep. As my brain finally turned off and I fell into a heavy slumber, I made the decision to deal with these problems in daylight.

The next morning, I decided that financial decisions were infinitely easier to make than emotional ones. It was time, I resolved, for Place de la Fontaine to be put up for sale.

CHAPTER FIFTEEN

A Venetian Wedding

After breakfast, the children and I took Raymond to the airport for his trip back to Sydney. As he walked through the departure gates there were no tears and no heavy heart. Our partings were becoming easier.

A quick bus ride took us to the TGV station at the other side of the sprawling airport. The TGV train arrived on time in Avignon; the other travellers looked daggers at me when I stood up refreshed from a heavy two-hour sleep. I noticed that the children had changed seats, pretending not to know me. What I did not know, but could guess, was that the snores and snuffles that I make when deeply asleep may have disturbed the quiet in the carriage. Raymond often compared the sounds emanating from my slumbers to those of a warthog. I am not sure that he has ever slept with a warthog to be qualified to judge. However, I was rejuvenated and ready to tackle all the problems that the season could throw at me. I wanted to immerse myself in my latest passion: writing.

My number one priority was to stave off bankruptcy; although it was not at the front door as yet, there were signs of it looking for me in my street. A tight rein on the budget, keeping paid help to the barest minimum, and not spending a Euro centime on any unnecessary work would be the key to keeping insolvency at bay.

Now that the agonising decision to sell Place de la Fontaine had been made, there were no buyers. The real estate market had not just gone flat; it had died a very quick death. French buyers were very thin on the ground due to the sluggish French economy, but this sort of property was the ideal second home for foreign holidaymakers. Taking a quick look around the supermarket car park showed that even in the height of summer, it was now mainly occupied by cars with number plates starting with a large F (signifying France), with few cars from other countries. They were mostly compact cars, too: Peugeots, Renaults or Citroëns. There were virtually no oversized four-wheel drives, as they are an economic impossibility with the spiralling cost of fuel in France. Conspicuous by their absence were the Germans with their large Mercedes and D for Deutschland embossed on their number plates, the English with GB for Great Britain, the Dutch with NL for the Netherlands. There were few

Italians and never any Spanish or Portuguese. As usual, there was a sprinkle of Belgians with their red and white number plates marked with a large B. The French say unkindly that in any road accident the chances are extremely high that a Belgian will be involved. I have learnt to give the Belgians a wide berth on the road just in case.

While helping me to load the car, Mimi asked why there were so many cars from the Czech Republic. 'Why on earth do you think that?' I replied, only half listening, desperately trying to remember if I had bought light bulbs, cakes of soap and white toilet paper for the Saturday changeover. 'The Czech Republic must be at least 1300 kilometres away. Do you remember when we drove to Venice and then on to Vienna? Well, it's even further. It would take more than twelve hours to do a trip like that. I don't think that many would come here.' Then the penny dropped, but Harry beat me to the punch. 'Oh, why are girls so dense? CH stands for *Confoederatio Helvetica*, which is the real name for Switzerland.'

Out of the mouths of babes. Of course the cars with CH belonged to the Swiss, who could whip down the expressway and be at our doorstep within four hours. More often than not, though, they were leaving their gold bars behind in the safe confines of Swiss banks. The Swiss were coming for holidays, not to buy a second home.

Traditionally, the biggest tourist slice in the Luberon goes to the Dutch and the Germans, who descend from the north in the hope of finding better weather and enjoying the culinary delights of Provence. The world economy was tightening, so buying a second home in Provence was the last thing on most tourists' minds. It was not easy to market Place de la Fontaine, given that inspections could only be done on Saturdays between midday and three o'clock, after the week's clients had left and everything had been cleaned and made ready for the next arrivals late in the afternoon. The problem did not lie there, though: no one, whatever the nationality, was interested.

~~~

I discovered during the tourist season that not many secrets of the clients escaped me — unfortunately. Claire cleaned the kitchen and bathrooms and I did the bedrooms. So it was my hand that went under the bed or under the mattress, and it was I who discovered that three people had been sleeping in one bed — but it was Claire who discovered that someone in the party had extremely long hair that had completely blocked the shower drain. Too often clients left bins overflowing, the fridge stuffed full of opened jams and yellowing and hardening cheeses. But it was the big surprises that were most distressing: the soup tureen still brimming with a combination of lentils and smelly sausage, or the baking dishes with burnt remnants of meat or rotting vegetables floating in a sea of olive oil that marked the clients' forays into French regional cuisine. Luckily, the vast majority of clients left the properties as requested, with the beds stripped, the linen in the large blue bags, the fridge empty and no bottles or garbage left lying around.

On Saturday afternoons when the cleaning had been finished and the first of many bales of washing was rumbling away in the workshop, Claire and I would sit outside in the shade of the persimmon tree and make up a list of the top ten qualities of our dream clients:

1. *Bald clients would be the best, as there would be no problems with the drains; preference was given to those who liked to wax every part of their body.*
2. *Gay men would be excellent because they were always tidy.*
3. *Oversexed clients would be great if they could all sleep in the same bed. This would save on the washing.*
4. *Dark-skinned people would be an advantage as it was impossible to remove instant summer tanning products from the white sheets and dressing gowns.*

5. *No babies because the cot is too difficult to pack away.*

6. *No friendly pets because they eat the stuffing from the sofas.*

7. *Only women who had natural hair colour because hair dye was difficult to remove from the white towels.*

8. *No smokers because they burn holes in the furniture and tablecloths.*

9. *Nobody who is in love, as they massage litres of scented oils into their partner's flesh, leaving stains that are impossible to remove from the sheets and mattresses.*

10. *Nobody who isn't in love, as they end their marriage or fight bitterly while on holiday, keeping the neighbours awake.*

We fell about laughing as we progressed through our demands for the Perfect Client. There was no room on our list for those who rang desperate for directions because they were stuck somewhere in the middle of page forty-five of the Michelin guide, or for those who were in St Saturnin les Avignon, a village over sixty kilometres away from St Saturnin les Apt. We had a wealth of anecdotes, some funny and some sad: the clients who came to celebrate forty years of friendship but had a roaring dispute on their first evening in Saignon, ending up with one couple taking the car

and leaving their former friends stranded; the bride
who rang in the middle of her honeymoon desperate
for something to read because she was unbelievably
bored; the well-known Australian clients who asked
for a ground sheet to be put across their bed for some
activity that remained nameless; the child who
accidentally locked herself in the bathroom; dealing
with broken teeth, infected insect bites and the
gynaecological problems that beset some women the
moment they stepped away from their home. Our list
was endless and we both knew that it would be added
to with every season.

~~~

I was in full swing writing my memoir, and a space on
the bottom shelf of the bookshelf had been cleared
ready for its much-anticipated arrival. During summer,
while the children were on the long school holidays,
the only time that the house was completely silent was
at four o'clock in the morning. I would put a load of
washing and the kettle on, read the main newspapers
from London, Paris and Sydney on the Internet and an
hour later force myself to be creative. Through a week's
trial of writing to a fixed program, I had discovered that
writing was extremely pleasurable but sitting in front of
a blank page was horrifying, especially first thing in the
morning. After two days I suspected that for me,

creativity only came if there was no alcohol in my system. After one week, I was positive; I could not drink one drop if I were to write at the pace I wanted. It was a huge incentive to write creatively and quickly.

Our house had so few rooms that I was forced to use a space in the living room as my office. The children pointed out to me that unless I gave them each a television for their bedroom we would have to share the space, so often I would be writing frantically while my children sat transfixed in front of SpongeBob SquarePants, the talking sponge, and his best friend Patrick the Starfish. The task was to write a minimum of 1000 words per day.

In the cool of the evening, I would sit with Zorro beside the Monet pond and read through my words — most of which were marked in red and consigned to the bin. If luck was going with me, I would manage to salvage 300 words, but often every sheet of paper had a large red pen mark zigzagging through it. It was depressing, but at the same time I was incapable of stopping. It was a long hard grind, as my mind took me back to places I never wanted to revisit. Inappropriate tears kept springing to my eyes. One minute I would be mid-flight talking to clients about what to do with their garbage, the next minute my eyes sprang a leak that would not stop. It was not just glistening moisture at the edges of my eyes. It was Niagara Falls, with the sounds effects from a horror film. Embarrassed, I would always claim some terrible allergic affliction that clogged my nose and made my eyes stream. I fooled no one.

My days were occupied with writing, washing and ironing sheets and trying in vain to train Zorro, who was becoming bigger by the day but was still completely untrained. Claire continued to give me good advice on his management, which I continued to ignore, even in the face of the number of shoes, mobile telephones, television controls, handbags or items of lingerie I lost as Zorro continued to create complete havoc. The huge mistake I had made by taking on a large dog, combined with a lack of training, was making the situation completely untenable. Sheets could no longer go on the line to be dried; in fact, nothing could go on the line. Zorro would leap up and drag item after item into the Monet pond until the lines were completely empty. The items that went first always belonged to me, but finally, through boredom, Zorro would take just about anything that wasn't nailed down. At night time he continued to dominate my life, scratching on the door and barking at unknown noises until I relented and allowed him in, whereupon he would take up residence on the leather sofas. Walks to neighbouring villages were meant to exhaust the young dog but afterwards he would snooze by my feet recuperating happily while I tried to continue to write yet another chapter, my legs aching. It was a total disaster of my own making.

At first Zorro was quite happy to bound up to the car when I opened the large electric gates to pass through into the garden. Then one day the unthinkable happened: he ran out, looked at me and continued to run. Five or six hours later he returned, barking at the gate waiting to enter. On talkback radio there had been endless discussions about people who abandoned their pets during the summertime or pets that were stolen while their owners were out. So when Zorro arrived home with a bedraggled little terrier cross that was evidently malnourished, unhappy and abandoned, my heart melted and I allowed the dog to stay until I could work out what to do with her. The following day Rosie — as I came to call her — had an epileptic fit and lay on the road frothing at the mouth and stiff as a board, so I did not doubt for a second that nobody loved this very unattractive dog. Zorro, however, was in love. His castration appeared to have been unsuccessful — he continued to wander, and Rosie certainly held his interest. The problem about what to do with the dog had to be resolved before the children arrived home from a short break with friends by the sea. They would think that it was a fine idea to keep the dog.

The postman cleared up the mystery one day when he asked me why Pearl was living with us when her real owner lived in the farmhouse behind the vines about 200 metres away, which we passed on our daily walk. So that was the reason behind Rosie's quickened pace. I was now more adept in my dealings with the Provençals, so it did not surprise me in the slightest when they began to tell me that Pearl (her real name) was a wonderful family pet and hunting dog. Naturally, they were prepared to negotiate a price for the animal. This stance changed radically when they realised that I had already visited the vet and the police about the forms required for the abuse of animal rights.

I look at her now, entwined in a black and white ball with Samba, our latest black cat, and think about the first few months we had her, when she would not even put her little paw inside the house, a place she had never been before. Things have changed. Rosie has her own pet chair beside the fire. Even though nowadays she sports a pink leather collar and a matching pink winter coat encrusted with diamantes, ribbons and bows that she wears for walks into the village to show that she is truly loved, she remains very ugly. My friends, the Wise Sages, said that Rosie would calm Zorro down and that his misdemeanours would decrease rapidly with her arrival. I'm still waiting. They continue to escape and spend their hours of freedom sitting beside the cheese vendor in the village on market day, in the hope of scoring some samples of his wares.

~~~

After the children's return from the seaside, we moved
into the latter part of summer and all that it entails:
finishing off incomplete kites and cubby houses, riding
bikes and revising last year's lessons with Claire in
preparation for the new school year, which starts the
first week of September. Coaching for Harry was
increased to a couple of hours per week with his
teacher and mentor, Madame George, who was
becoming more demanding as Harry's capabilities
increased. The book lists had been received and over
two hours had been spent in the large office supply
store in the north of Avignon collecting the regulation
colour exercise books with matching coloured plastic
protective covers. They had to have the correct size,
colour and type of paper. The different types and sizes
of squared lined paper that were used by the French
bewildered me but not the children, who understood
the nuances of the little squares. The book list included
a pen list with detailed quantities of the correct
assortment of coloured pens: red, black, blue and green.
All were thrown into our trolley. Different fountain
pens with appropriate refill ink cartridges had to be
bought. Long and erudite discussions about the types of
nib took place between the two budding scholars. The
list was endless and confusing but Mimi and Harry
seemed to know what was required of them for their
schooling needs, so I stood waiting patiently with
money in hand, ready to do my part of the transaction.

In September, Mimi would be entering her second year of high school and Harry would be in his last year of primary school. It barely seemed possible that these Australian children had made such a quantum leap in culture and language and nowadays straddled the two worlds with such ease. Mimi continued to read a huge variety of styles of literature, mostly in English, but like her friends at school she was coping with the large extracts from classic French novels that were on the required reading list. My admiration for both of my children was boundless as they overcame the difficulties of the French language that I had struggled with in my third year of university. Nothing fazed them as they rose to the challenge of learning long lists of irregular verbs and differences in tenses. The French education system is obsessed with language and it is drilled day after day; dictations are still very much part of the syllabus. It made our lackadaisical Australian attitude to the English language seem very much below par. During the short period of time that I taught languages in Sydney in the 1980s, the task was nearly impossible; none of the students had ever been taught English grammar so their knowledge of verbs and sentence construction was extremely poor and needed to be built up before they could make the first steps to understanding a foreign language.

Claire was also gratified by her offspring's successes. The French education system often has entrance exams for universities and selected private schools and courses that are attempted after the completion of the *baccalauréat*. Her daughters had received their results from these highly competitive exams, which they had taken in June, at the end of the scholastic year. The results were a triumph for both girls. Géraldine, whose speciality was mathematics, was accepted into a strenuous course that would give her a wealth of choices in her future career. Her younger sister Lorélie had competed against thousands of young hopefuls to gain entrance into the prestigious naval officers' school in Brest. The odds were stacked against her: the enormous size of the candidature was bad enough, but being a female seemed an insurmountable disability. Not only had she been accepted — she was also one of the strongest candidates.

It was an outstanding achievement — directly for both the girls and indirectly for Claire. She had weathered a bitter divorce that had left her with crippling financial constraints, and had had no family to help her for many years, until she had met Patrick with his fabulous handlebar moustache and heart of gold. She had managed to keep the girls on a straight path, reciting the family mantra that education and good manners were the only things that mattered. It certainly helped that Claire was gorgeous and intelligent and the girls had inherited her brains and her beauty. Needless to say, Géraldine and Lorélie had both been at the top of their class most of their lives. Magic surrounded Claire and her home, woven in a tight blanket over her family and all those who touched her life. However, Claire was like many French nowadays and kept religion at a safe distance. Their home was completely bereft of any religious icons, crosses or statues. She attested that within the home she maintained a strong belief in what is right and wrong and had no need for religious symbols.

It always startled me to see such a radical shift in viewpoint in a relatively short period of time. When I lived in France during the late 1970s, religion was an integral part of the social fabric: discreet crosses hung around necks, saint days were respected and traditions upheld, religious symbols were scattered throughout the home and social interaction was strongly entwined with Mass on Sunday and the other holy days sprinkled thickly through the French calendar. Almost thirty years later, there appears to be a marked change in the religious life of the French: they still keep the public holidays but don't necessarily observe their religious significance.

~~~

The lack of clients towards the end of October allowed us to take advantage of the frequent flyer points that had accumulated once again, and we set off for yet another flying visit to Sydney to see family and friends. We all wondered secretly if this eternal travelling was giving anyone a great deal of pleasure. When would we ever be able to go to Morocco, Turkey or New York on the cheap package trips leaving from Marseille? In Sydney in October and November, the children's old friends were in school and friendships were fast becoming forgotten. My old friends, too, were busy with their lives, and in retrospect even Raymond seemed bizarrely distracted and preoccupied. Part of the puzzle was not fitting together. Why does a woman choose not to see what is right under her nose?

Raymond was coming to France in early 2004 so we could have a family holiday, hopefully with nuptials included, in Venice during the February school holidays. As yet there had not really been any concrete proposal, but I had visited a lot of 'weddings in Italy' sites on the Internet, so I was more than prepared. Outstanding idea. Excellent. Perfect. The children would come with us and we could spend a week floating in a gondola in the freezing cold and driving rain and slop around ankle-deep in the flooded St Mark's Square. It would be so romantic. It could not get better than that.

I would have stopped talking about our wonderful wedding-to-be if I had noticed his fingernails turning white as he gripped the armchair in total terror.

CHAPTER SIXTEEN

The Bottom of Things

November in France is usually rainy, cold and miserable, and 2003 was no exception. The properties were closed for minor repairs. The school routine had been quickly picked up again through necessity, as the piles of homework grew daily.

Raymond had finally said just before we left Sydney that February was unsuitable for a winter wedding as it would coincide with another huge family gathering in New Zealand, and he felt that as we had waited so many years a couple of months more didn't matter. Maybe we should wait for a more suitable time for everyone? I did not notice his shifty eyes and sweaty palms or his inability to look at me directly. Venice in midwinter was perhaps not the best choice. It wasn't a bad one as far as I was concerned, but he did have his reasons and family is important. The impending nuptials were put on hold and I turned my attention to seeing if I could get my manuscript read by someone in publishing, printed and then sold in every major bookshop in the world.

The manuscript completed, I assumed that it was only a question of time before some ecstatic publisher would come knocking at my door waving a massive cheque under my nose. Only a good dose of reality could burst the bubble and I steadfastly refused to listen to anything that resembled it. Not once had I stopped to think that less than two per cent of aspiring writers actually have manuscripts published. As usual, I had gone about it completely the wrong way, never bothering to find out the basics — how to present the manuscript, what type or what spacing to use, should it be bound or not bound — let alone heeding any suggestions from family friends who were published authors. Enveloped in a cloud of idyllic ignorance, I made a list of important things to do:

1. *Review manuscript once again.*
2. *Write fabulous letter to publisher or agent.*
3. *Find out who was a fabulous publisher or agent.*
4. *Decide how many noughts I would accept as a contract.*
5. *Decide how many noughts I would accept for film rights.*

Hours were spent on the Internet, double-checking any information on publishing, as well as gleaning any information I could from prefaces and acknowledgments of books in the desperate search for a name to whom I could direct my manuscript or letters. The task of sourcing names and addresses of publishers and agents from all parts of the English-speaking world was eventually achieved, then the long process of printing portions or sample chapters with an accompanying letter began, absorbing reams of paper and black ink. Hours were spent standing in queues at the village post office, paying vast sums of money for postage to faraway destinations; no country was going to avoid my deluge of appeals for publication. In descending priority, large thick creamy envelopes were posted to every major publishing house in the English-speaking world, then to medical publications, scientific journals, legal periodicals, newspapers, travel magazines, women's magazines, new mother magazines and finally airline magazines, even though my manuscript did not fit their submission guidelines. I was convinced that they would see the value and quality of my manuscript and immediately change their editorial direction. Some were sent only my fabulous letter, written entirely for their benefit; one sheet of creamy deckle paper, designed to make them drop everything and beat a path to my door, waving wads of money in front of my face. Others were sent the fabulous letter with bonus extracts from my manuscript, mentioning my immediate availability to discuss fat cheques and film options. Ignorance was bliss, and on a cold winter's afternoon, the idea of a fat cheque was so appealing and comforting.

On another front, I began the embarrassing undertaking of calling agents in London. They were, for the most part, polite, but clear that they were not in the market for yet another aspiring author, especially one from the Antipodes. Some were gracious and spent a few moments of their precious time directing me to another area — well away from them.

The children sat quietly munching their afternoon snack as we went through the pile of letters that began to arrive before Christmas. At first, they were convinced that if I said something would happen, it generally did. We waited patiently for the letter that would say that a publisher wanted to see the manuscript in its entirety or would like our address so that they could send a truckload of money to the house before Christmas. When Mimi and Harry started to avoid afternoon snacks, preferring to make a beeline to their rooms to begin their hours of homework, I questioned how realistic I was with my goal, despite the enthusiasm my friends and family had shown about what I believed to be the final draft of my precious manuscript.

During our daily telephone calls, Raymond stood fast in his conviction that it would be published sooner or later; the emphasis was on the sooner, so he said. However, this seemed to be the only area where there was any agreement between us. Our daily calls had become even more spasmodic and curt. The publication of my book was the only subject where we could voice our opinions without disputes. I trod carefully around other subjects, never asking any questions that would lead to answers I did not want to acknowledge. Emails were sent to the children, but nothing came to me. Our relationship appeared to have sprung a major leak, and yet I doggedly maintained that a wedding would fix everything. Claire never ventured to voice her opinion out loud, but she often swung her right arm limply in front of me, leaving me in no doubt that she thought it was time for amputation, not a wedding. I knew deep down that she was right, but I couldn't bring myself to voice my fears.

After a very quiet and fairly glum Christmas, the three of us voted that it was our Worst Ever and we all took the vote never to repeat the experience of a small Christmas. Great food and loads of presents did not compensate for the lack of guests and noise that is necessary for a festive occasion. After Claire and Patrick's family and friends had left their tiny house there was room for us at the table to celebrate New Year with them, but most of the holidays were spent lying in front of the television or reading books in front of the fire in quiet boredom. The children charged back to school the moment the holidays were over, desperate to be reunited with their friends. I promised them that we would do something fabulous during the next holidays.

Claire suggested that a change of scene was in order for the forthcoming February school holidays, in an effort to shake me from my disenchantment with fate and destiny. Bob and Marie Sharp, Australian friends of my parents, had lived in Florence for over thirty years. They, very wisely I thought, spent a great deal of the miserable Florentine winter enjoying the affections of grandchildren and a Sydney summer, so they offered me the use of their wonderful apartment, right on the Arno River in the heart of Florence. Claire and Raphaël would join us; Claire had found a small bed and breakfast near the Sharps' apartment, on the opposite side of the Piazza Santa Croce. From Apt to Florence it would take seven hours in the car to travel 670 kilometres and cost ninety euros in diesel and tolls. With Claire at the wheel, we would get there in record time. She had spent a great deal of her young married life driving in the sand hills of Djibouti in eastern Africa, so I always caved in to her requests to be the driver. As it happened, that was a good thing when we spun out of control down the expressway, unexpected snow thick all around us and black ice on the road. We joined most of the cars on the expressway, which had skidded into the ditches along the side of the road before the Autoroute du Soleil was closed by the authorities. The car aquaplaned to the shoulder of the expressway, where we stayed for an eternity in our white cocoon until the snowplough rescued us. Above us was a large billboard: 'Welcome to the Sunny south of France, where the sun always shines.'

So began the trip of a lifetime. Travel has always been such a part of my life that it is an experience in itself to be with someone like Claire, who (apart from her African travels as a young woman) had rarely been out of Provence, let alone France. For her, suitcases were about moving house yet again as the family's circumstances were continually downgraded: rarely for the joys of a holiday. This holiday was to be savoured, devoured, grabbed with two hands and consumed with gusto. Claire was not a woman who politely nibbled at life; she had it by the throat and was attacking it without constraint. Research had been done on every facet of the history and culture of Florence; opening and closing times for every conceivable gallery and museum within a sixty-kilometre radius had been checked and then double-checked on the Internet, maps drawn, guide books consulted and basic Italian phrases from tapes learnt parrot fashion. Having spent a great deal of time in Florence as a young woman, I could guide everyone in and out of the back streets to avoid the hordes of tourists that stuck to the main tracks around the large tourist spots. I had never been so ready for a holiday.

All of the museums were visited. The dancing Botticelli ladies that had so delighted Harry when he first saw them four years ago were in the same place in the Uffizi Art Gallery and looked just as beautiful, but this time, with the wisdom of his eleven years, he suddenly found it bitterly sad that he was growing older but they would always remain the same. Shoes, bags and cheap belts were bought from the markets in Siena; every flavour of ice cream was tried and assessed on its merits; luxurious mink coats were admired in the exclusive shop windows of Fendi and Gucci; items with Ferrari insignia were drooled over by the boys while Claire and I admired the Alessi kitchenware, even though little was bought. Our visits to the local shops and markets ended with us staggering away with woven straw baskets filled to the brim with freshly made ravioli stuffed with fresh ricotta cheese and spinach, sticks of salami, large wedges of pale hard Parmesan or Pecorino cheeses, and the ubiquitous plastic containers of olives marinated in rosemary and garlic.

In the back streets of Florence, we went in search of restaurants only frequented by the locals and stumbled upon places that offered up thick garlicky soups filled with cabbage, beans and vegetables, grilled meats liberally sprinkled with herbs, and boiled meat dishes served with a vivid green herb sauce that was astutely side-stepped by the children, who screwed their faces up in mock horror. They preferred to savour instead the huge diversity of pasta dishes and thick tomato-based stews made by grandma out the back, who served up the requested dishes while still stirring the pot of bubbling polenta — a thick corn meal — which serves as an accompaniment to many Tuscan meals. If there were any room left, and there always was, the dessert list was attacked as if there were no tomorrow: apple tarts, ice creams, slices of sponge cakes oozing cream and chocolate topped with almonds and meringue, all made by grandma. Nothing would stop the three ravenous adolescents.

Claire and I pretended to be pillars of restraint but tumbled pathetically when it came to the local varieties of red wine and the hard sweet nut biscuits that went with the fortified digestives. A competition was started to find a loaf that personified the perfect consistency and shape of Italian bread, but we voted unanimously that the French won hands down in this lone area. And while we waited in queues, Claire drilled the children in French irregular verbs, tenses and spelling, much to the great amusement of American tourists. The Italians might have fabulous architecture and outstanding art galleries, but nothing in the world will ever compare with the beauty of the French language, according to the children's private tutor.

Travelling with Claire was like travelling with a frenzied whirlwind; she was so excited about the differences between French and Italian architecture, the language, and the nonstop vibrancy of the Italian way of life. Her enthusiasm fuelled us in moments of pathetic tiredness and overcame our dismay when we had to climb yet another tower or more endless flights of stairs leading to a spectacular view. And up we went: up the 463 steps of the Brunelleschi Duomo in Florence, along the 4.2 kilometres of walls around Lucca, up the tallest tower in San Gimignano — 54 metres high — which in the end did not even compete with the *Torre del Mangia* in Siena at 102 metres high and with 505 steps.

Somewhere in the middle of Florence I caught myself in a daydream, wandering through the same streets and emotions as twenty years before: the same emotional turmoil and with the same man. But the iron grip that Raymond had had around my heart was loosening just a little. Why was it not possible to have all areas of my life under control? I tried to make a list of positive things in my life:

1. *Mimi and Harry were in robust health, happy and wise beyond their years.*
2. *Clients were coming back to Provence in droves.*
3. *The manuscript was finished, even though the wonderful cathartic effect I had hoped for never eventuated.*
4. *My business would survive another year as I staved off bankruptcy once again.*

For the first time my lists did not work. Basically I was unhappy. It was February 2004; our winter wedding should have taken place in Venice but here I was in Florence with my best friend and the children. I wanted to run away as far as possible and not face the reality of what was happening.

～～

Our bags were barely unpacked from Florence when the telephone rang. It was Lizzie: 'Henrietta, have you heard the news?' She was always the first to know everything. 'The March school excursion for Venice and Ravenna has just been cancelled due to terrorist alerts. The kids will be so disappointed. The school will not risk it, but what if we do it ourselves? Do you think that you could manage to get away for a couple of days in mid-April before the season gets under way? Really, what are the chances that there will be a terrorist strike in Venice? What do you think? Let's pack the kids in the cars and head off to Italy. Just the five kids and us. I'll find the accommodation. Let's go. What do you say?'

What could I say? Yeah, sure — and hey, that's a great place to have a wedding! Pity Raymond doesn't want to attend his own fucking ceremony. I couldn't bring myself to tell her that I never wanted to go to Venice again in my life. That April coincides with the anniversary of the death of my husband, when normally I take to my bed in tears with boxes of tissues to wait out the day. Instead I heard my voice reply meekly: 'Sure. Let's use the long weekend to go to Venice.'

All I really wanted was to float down the canal in Raymond's arms in a sea of love that had not gone bitter and twisted.

Our backpacks packed once again, we threw them, along with the dogs, into the back of the car, dropping Zorro and Rosie off at the kennels. It would take eight hours to travel the 720 kilometres to Venice. It was safer to cut the journey in half, setting off at five o'clock, the moment afternoon classes at the high school ended, so that we could stop at a hotel near Nice airport. We would have an evening picnic in Nice and then start very early the next morning to attack the myriad tunnels into Italy. As evening descended on Nice, tablecloths, wooden boards and knives, picnic glasses and plates appeared from our hampers and there we sat, glasses in hand, listening to the ebullient sounds of happy children munching on a mouth-watering roast chicken banquet, with cheeses, fruit, baguettes, chocolate desserts and copious bottles of lemonade, Perrier and red wine. Despite my reservations, our trip was off to a wonderful start.

We spent an idyllic three days floating on gondolas, eating ice creams and staying up far too late. The pale rays from the mid-April sun moved across the lagoon of Venice but nothing eclipsed the sunny moments that we spent together as we lavished attention and love on our children. Louie and Ollie were delightful in their enthusiasm, as was little Margaux, who was becoming a young person in her own right. My children suddenly realised that she was no longer just a little dot who would fall asleep in her mother's arms at the end of the evening. She was there to play and be counted in on all of their games. In three days we traversed Venice by foot or by boat or gondola so many times that we began to look like locals as the children wove their way instinctively through the throngs of bedazzled tourists, bumping our little hand-pulled trolley up and down the steps and stone pathways of Venice. We had thick frothy coffees while the children ate cakes; we devoured picnics on the island of Burano, with its colourful painted houses; we basked in the watery sun, kicked balls and once again licked ice creams.

Blissful perfect days. As they say, the calm before the storm. When we walked through St Mark's Square for the last time, the Venetian authorities were hurrying to put down the planks in readiness for the unseasonable and quite ferocious flooding that was imminent, ready to dampen the tourists' spirits and feet.

On our return, I needed to confront Raymond with my fears: was he involved with another person? The answer to this question was finally obvious to me. I just needed confirmation. My father Jack would no longer listen to any sentence that had Raymond's name in it and my closest ally, my sister Kate, was not too far behind. Apparently, everyone except me knew what was happening. As it often is the way, I was left fumbling in the dark, not really wanting to open my eyes because that is when I would have to take some sort of action.

Love is blind, as they say, but not deaf. When telephone calls started to come in the middle of the night and no messages were left, and worse still when messages were left containing hysterical and abusive diatribes from a very deranged and nasty woman, it was time for damage control. It was unsettling that this unstable person had access to my telephone numbers. With bile and spite colouring her words, the woman left me in no doubt that she was in a relationship with Raymond and wanted me to know.

Excluding the time leading up to and during my marriage of eight years, I had spoken, written or emailed to Raymond nearly every week, and often daily, for over twenty-two years, but now the knives were out, the gloves were off. We had been very careful about never mixing our lives together; no communal addresses, bank accounts or children. He lived on his side of the line and the children and I lived on ours. Admittedly, I had taken my line a little further by going to France. Words such as 'betrayal' and 'vengeance' began to sprinkle our conversations and emails. Poison filled every nook and cranny of our relationship.

Misunderstandings from twenty years previously began to resurface, as they never had been clearly dealt with and dispatched to the dusty vaults where they belonged. Grievances and disappointments swirled around, sucking us down into the vortex of despair. For the first time, Mimi and Harry watched, powerless to help as their pillar of strength and determination disintegrated before their eyes. Claire, too, stood by and for the first time said nothing. Having experienced an acrimonious divorce first-hand, she was aware that only time would allow the crisis to develop fully and explode — and after that, some sort of help could be offered, to clean away the detritus.

'Go back to Sydney. I will look after the children. You cannot do this over the telephone. It must be face to face.' Claire had given me the green light that I had been waiting for. Within half an hour, I had thrown a couple of T-shirts, underwear, toothbrush and a huge selection of books into my large handbag and walked out the door, hoping to buy a ticket to Sydney on any airline that had an available seat when I reached the airport in Paris. Claire had said to take two weeks but I knew that one would be more than enough. May was a busy time with the properties. I could miss one Saturday but not two. Mimi and Harry heaved a long sigh of relief. They always missed me, but anything was better than living with me right now, with the perpetual thundercloud over my head.

Something that my mother Sheilagh used to say finally reached me loud and clear in my dreams: 'At the bottom of everything there is usually a bottom'. I wanted to prove my mother wrong even from beyond the grave, even though I knew beyond a doubt that there was another woman involved — a woman I called The Nasty One. What I did not know was how important she was to Raymond.

Raymond had shifty eyes and a blank dead-mullet look when I approached this subject, spitting words at him like missiles: 'I have just spent twenty-four hours sitting in a plane to fly out here to speak to you and all you can say is that I am overreacting! I just want the truth. I want to know what is going on. Do you understand that you are mixing me up with your affairs? Do you realise that this Nasty One is leaving obscene messages on my telephone in the middle of night? Did you realise that the Nasty One has been reading my manuscript that you must have left lying around your office? That manuscript was for your eyes only, not some bimbo who you picked up. Raymond, finally it is over. No more. We are finished. I am too tired to listen to your excuses. We are too geographically challenged, but more to the point, I don't want to fight for you any more. Raymond, I don't love you any more. I have no respect for you. Do what you wish with this bimbo, it really doesn't concern me — but as choices go, she seems irresponsible, nasty and cruel. I doubt if she will make you very happy. And by the way, I am going to Manly Police Station to give them the dates and times that she has rung me and details of what was said, and if I receive any more calls I will be taking out an apprehended violence order against her. Don't think that I am joking. She has approached my family and I will protect us. This must stop. I hope you understand.'

I felt ill. My self-esteem had taken a beating. The police had explained that it was out of their control to stop someone making international calls to France, but they put the complaint into their report. I had never wanted our relationship to end in this manner, but now there was no turning back.

CHAPTER SEVENTEEN

You've Got Mail!

The days after the break-up with Raymond were spent shattered with jet lag and despair, waiting for the plane to take me back to France and my children. I walked the streets of my childhood in Mosman and along the Sydney beaches, deep in murderous thought about the pitfalls of true love. While on the foreshores of the sandy beach in front of Manly Wharf, I heard a jumble of sounds resembling a name. Against the strong wind, I heard 'Miss ...' but the rest of the name was eaten up in the wind. Looking up, I saw that there were few people on the beach. In May it was possible to enjoy the last remnants of the autumn sunshine. A young mother with six small children appeared to be waving to someone near me but I did not recognise her, so I continued on my way until the incessant calling and waving made me stop to take another look at the young mother.

'It's me. Catherine Turnbull. Don't you remember

me?' It was difficult to lie barefacedly but she obviously knew me well, so I leapt in the deep end: 'Catherine, of course I recognise you. Why, you haven't changed one bit since we last saw each other!' If only I could remember when we had met each other last.

She was a very enthusiastic woman with arms waving, grabbing escaping children as we spoke. 'Heavens, are all these your children?' Two of them looked very similar. 'Are they all twins?' What kind of demented woman would keep having children after the first two sets of twins? Was she going to populate Australia by herself?

'Are you joking? Four of them are mine and two belong to that couple over there by the water's edge. Neither David nor I had twins, which is strange, because it tends to run in the family.'

She had told me the key words to decipher the puzzle. She and her twin brother David had been the top students of their year when I had taught French and Italian in a Sydney high school for a brief period during the early 1980s. They were both charming, clever and extremely serious students. Catherine's determination made her stand out from the rest of the students in her year. Nothing would have changed very much, although I guessed four young children would test her limits. Having learnt to be a little more wily when it comes to inviting near-strangers into my house, I assessed the situation and reckoned that with four small children, European travel would not be on the cards.

'Catherine, it is a pleasure to meet you again. You must come and visit me if you are ever in France. I really do mean it.' Her face exploded with mirth as she began digging into her voluminous bag for a pen and paper to write down my details, squealing with delight.

'You wouldn't believe it but I am due to go to England and America for a conference later this month or early June.' I shook my head in utter disbelief. Once again Mimi would have to vacate her room and sleep with me so that our guest could sleep in a modicum of comfort. How on earth could I rescind my invitation when this young woman wanted to travel so far out of her way just to come to visit me? I counted on the fact that it would be too difficult to coordinate and a terrible inconvenience for such a short trip. My addled brain filed the information away, safe in the knowledge that she would never come, or so I hoped.

Four days later, still jet-lagged and a great deal poorer, I returned home to France with some of my self-respect still intact. During the first five months of 2004, I had been in Venice, Florence and now Sydney for less than five days. My head was spinning; I had no idea what time zone, day or country I was in except that I was home. It was better to be alone with children, cats and dogs and a struggling business than to be treated badly by a man. Winter wedding plans had become annihilation plans, verging on the homicidal. On my return home, I did the adult thing and erased Raymond's email address, threw out all of his clothes from the cupboard and told the children never to mention his name again.

~~~

Both Mimi and Harry stood back waiting for the storm to clear and for me to right myself so we could return to our normal routine. But nothing would shake me from my intense depression. The season was well and truly underway, and Claire was carrying the load. She kept checks on the linen supply, making sure that the washing and ironing were up to date. The lights in our workshop would go on at five o'clock, but instead of working alongside Claire I buried myself under the bedclothes, wanting the world to stop. I was neglecting my children, my friends and my clients. I was wretched; acting like a teenager with a broken heart — or maybe like a woman with shattered dreams on the verge of divorce? One day Claire slipped into the house to wave her magic wand and when I finally emerged from the bedroom, I found that the house was clean and tidy, the oven sparkling, and salads prepared and laid out on freshly ironed tablecloths. A note written in thick bold strokes had more than a touch of the imperative:

Henrietta ~
Love him forever in a corner of your heart but it's time to
let him go. Learn to use your left hand.
Claire (your right-hand man!)

Once again she was right. Freedom was the most
important thing to me and for too long I had made
excuses. Love can be nurtured, but once it is dead, a
woman must turn the page.

Much to my surprise, Catherine Turnbull contacted
me barely ten days later. Somehow she was determined
to spend a thirty-six hour leave period from her tight
schedule with my family and me in the Luberon. Her
guest lecture on directions for Sydney healthcare and
social services was scheduled for Monday lunchtime in
Cambridge, which would give her just enough time to
get to us on the fast train from Paris, see every village
and tourist spot between Avignon and Apt on the way
from the train station, have dinner, early bed, early
morning trip to the market at the world-renowned Isle
sur la Sorge, then back to the station to catch the train
that would take her all the way to London, where she
could catch yet another train to get her close to
Cambridge, where a bus would take her to her final
destination. Evidently, Catherine's fortitude had not
waned in the passing years.

I was becoming increasingly accustomed to distant

acquaintances making the pilgrimage across vast distances just to experience our little corner of the world even for the shortest of trips. When the weather was warm, our house seemed to have revolving doors as acquaintances, friends and family made full use of our hospitality. Every year, the children would listen dutifully to my promise that I would put on the brakes during the season and we would entertain fewer guests. They rolled their eyes skyward as they knew that this would not come to pass. I found it irresistible to catch up with people from my past and from our part of the world, to hear the long flat Australian vowels and the laconic wit. It was revitalising to listen to their slant on European travel, and often I gained a fresh insight on my routine life from the perspective of holidaymakers.

Catherine's train had barely left the station when my telephone rang, deep within my bottomless bag. I knew that it would be clients to announce their arrival, as the season was now in full swing. It was Dr Porter with his wife, Amanda, who were on holidays with three other couples to celebrate their fiftieth birthdays. Dr Porter had been my obstetrician for both of my pregnancies and had showed me great compassion during the time my husband Norman was dying. Somehow our paths had crossed many times over the years, even once by accident on the Spanish Steps in Rome. He and his companions wanted to celebrate their half-centuries with a quick trip to Italy and France, spending a week in Saignon to relax, enjoy the food and wine and, more importantly, unwind from their busy lives. They were no longer hell-raisers but they called their three-week European tour their 'L' Raisers Tour. This meant nothing to me until Harry pointed out the obvious: 'Don't you get it, *Maman*? "L" is fifty in Roman numerals.' Sometimes it is easier when it is spelt out to you by a nearly twelve-year-old.

The moment the telephone rang and I heard the voices in the background screaming in delight that everything was perfect, I could guess that their unwinding process was already in motion. The chaos of the season was unfolding.

My head was almost clear from jet lag by now but my heart was still heavy from emotion. Life continued and so did the May mortgage repayments, which due to an error out of my control weren't paid on time. A hurried meeting with Monsieur Perrard was organised. Claire offered to come with me, thinking that I was incapable of making any financial decision in my current state. She was privy to most of my affairs, but there were some things that I liked to keep private.

Monsieur Perrard began our meeting with a short black coffee in the café next door to his office, but no longer accompanied by several cigarettes. The cigarette packets were gone, along with his famous upward-pointing moustache. His eyes shone with compassion as we started thrashing out solutions. The bottom line was that I was so overextended that something had to give. An oversight between banks had delayed my transactions and therefore the funds were not in the correct account on the correct day. Monsieur Perrard had been saying the same words since I had bought the Wild Thyme Patch: I was perilously overextended, precariously living from month to month, juggling accounts. Finally he said the words that had been in my head for too long. Should I not consider selling the family home in Sydney? Where did I consider home? I knew that Daniel was right, but it had taken me so long to come to terms with selling Place de la Fontaine. My timing for that sale could not have been worse. By the time I finally made the decision to sell, not one buyer could be found. The real estate market in Provence had fallen completely flat and Place de la Fontaine was still on the market. The same could not be said for the real estate market in Sydney, which was going through yet another record boom. Prices were skyrocketing. If I could find enough space in my head, I knew that I would have to give it due consideration.

We were moving into the best time of the year — the soft sun of May. Field after field of wheat was electric yellow, stained with red poppies in irregular aureoles. Within six weeks, these same fields of waving golden wheat would have the colour stripped from their stalks, which would turn a sun-bleached white when the crops were harvested into large bales ready for use. The frilly petals of the irises, ranging from soft lilacs and mauves to deep magentas and aubergines, emerged in such casual beauty from the wild grasses along the banks of our country roads. The poppies and irises springing up everywhere contrasted sharply with the uniformity of the straight lines of the cherry trees in the surrounding orchards, already shining with red pendulous globes. How such beauty continues to flourish and triumph following winter after harsh winter is astounding.

However, among all of this beauty, I just wanted to lie down and die. Money, or rather the lack of it, was consuming my every thought and yet I couldn't come to the decision that I should sell the house in Sydney. At the back of my mind, there had always been the possibility of returning to Sydney for the children's final years of schooling — or back into the arms of Raymond. The children were more than happy to stay in France for their education and Raymond had thrown his arms around someone else. But selling the house was such a final action. Pots and pans flew around the kitchen as I took out my aggression and inability to make a decision. The children avoided me like the plague, as did Claire, who had enough sense to know that the storm would pass. Nothing was going the way I wanted. There was:

1. *No love in my life.*
2. *No buyer for Place de la Fontaine.*
3. *No interest in the manuscript.*

4. *No decision about the family home in Sydney.*
5. *No money to pay for the mortgages.*

Claire and I sat down one afternoon with paper and pen and worked out the urgency of the financial situation and what solutions could be found, if any. We were both horrified but not surprised when we calculated exactly how much money was required to keep the business turning per month. My father was unable to help, and even if he could, I just couldn't bring myself to ask. Raymond was out of the question. Other members of the family were out of the question. Somewhere the solution was there; I just had to shake myself out of my lethargy and start thinking.

At three o'clock one night as my liver tried vainly to process another attack of alcohol, it came to me: the stock market. I had had the good fortune to make a nest egg in early 2000 and then sell everything just before a dramatic correction in the market. I knew that I would never have the gumption to go down that path again; once was more than enough. But I could sell anything that remained in my name. That would give me a little bit of breathing space. I rang a broker in Sydney and began the arrangements. The second call to Sydney was to the real estate office, to say that I had made up my mind that I wanted a spring sale for the family home. I was completely gutted, but the focus was coming back. There were two priorities:

1. *Happy children.*
2. *A successful business.*

The children were delightful and happy. Interim school report cards had come in and they were both glowing in all areas. Financially I could hold out until the beginning of 2005 if I sold all of the shares that I had put aside in an emergency fund, by which time the family home would be sold. On the emotional front, tears continued to spring up unexpectedly. I did not want to admit that Claire was perhaps correct in her assessment of the breakup that my pride was hurt more than anything. Proud, vain and lazy — I had the trifecta in life.

By the end of May, nothing had happened with the manuscript. Letters of refusal continued to arrive periodically but the deluge had ebbed. The manuscript itself began to gather dust at the bottom of the bookshelf. My birthday was coming up in the first week in June and little was going to help lift the cloud of doom and gloom. Destiny obviously was not going my way this year.

My forty-sixth birthday started off badly, with poor calculations of my exact age. Giggling at my inability to subtract 1958 from 2004, Mimi and Harry sat on my bed, which was covered with presents that they had chosen with Claire or had painstakingly made themselves with a needle and thread. I couldn't even feel any joy when I realised I had miscalculated my age and I was younger than I thought. It was only when I went to the computer to check the incoming emails that my heart really soared and I screamed with delight: one of the biggest publishing companies in Sydney was interested in my manuscript. It defied belief. My birthday was starting to look better by the moment.

Waiting for me to grace the workroom with my presence, Claire had started work, trying to keep up with the colossal task of washing and ironing the sheets for the three properties. This day was no different and she was up to her elbows sorting out coloured towels from fluffy white dressing gowns with pockets full of used tissues left by the clients.

'Come quick. You must look at something that has arrived in the computer. Come quick. Drop all of that.' By this stage tears were streaming down everyone's faces. I was screaming for joy.

'They are going to publish it. I've done it. Do you know what this means?'

Claire too, was busy wiping away her tears. 'This is so *fantastique*. You must go with the children to Sydney to sign the contract.'

We were in the middle of the season, all the houses were occupied nonstop, the washing and ironing was unrelenting as were the temperatures that were already pushing past thirty-seven degrees, building up to an early hot summer. It was the worst possible time to leave Claire to deal with everything by herself. Even with Claire's immense capacity for hard work, this would take her to the limits. My fingers were crossed that I would be able to find someone to help. Maybe Fabienne would be able to find the time? Claire looked extremely doubtful. Fabienne, the young girl who often came to work as an extra pair of hands on Saturday, was working nonstop in the fields as the harvests were in full swing.

Within the space of an hour, after a restorative cup of tea beside the pond, I worked out exactly what I should do. Fly to Sydney to sign the contract, taking with me Mimi, Harry and also Raphaël, as both boys would still be under twelve and for the last time they would qualify for a child's fare — in fact, we would be home two days before Raphaël turned twelve. It was an opportunity of a lifetime for him although it would be extremely hard for him to be away from his family. We would be heading into winter, not necessarily the time to show off the best of Sydney to our young tourist. Claire, Patrick and Fabienne pulled the short straw and would be left to carry the heavy load of cleaning, washing and ironing and dealing with all of the ongoing problems associated with the three properties, keeping the two poorly behaved dogs in line, and also the two cats, and a small rodent problem in the garage that wasn't worth thinking about.

Harry was more concerned about how the oft-mentioned truckload of cash would find its way to our house or how the very fat cheque would squeeze through the letterbox.

Frantic calls to airlines to try to secure seats for the day that school finished turned out to be fruitless, as there was a general exodus from Paris on the first day of the long summer holidays. As always, it was the Saturday changeover day that was presenting me with problems: I needed a Sunday flight returning by Friday a week later, which was proving to be impossible. I decided to take the children out of school early. Letters were written to the school explaining the situation and asking for five days' leave of absence, which was unwillingly granted. We were not sure how I would be replaced for the one or two Saturdays for bed making and cleaning duties; on at least one occasion, Patrick would be donning my apron and joining Claire and Fabienne.

One of the airlines came through with the seats — and better still, there was a chance that the thousands of frequent flyer points that I had recently accumulated could be used as an upgrade to business class for a portion of the trip. We would be away seventeen days. The ink on the departure stamp was barely dry from my quick trip in May but it was a dream come true for everyone. Raphaël had never been in a large plane, let alone one that would take him to the other side of the world where he would have to speak English with everyone except us. His first experience of travel had been our trip to Florence earlier in the year and now he was off to Sydney. He was spinning with excitement.

CHAPTER EIGHTEEN

The Fat Lady Sings

Paris was warm and balmy, heralding the beginning of yet another hot summer's day while we stood in the queue for two hours waiting to have our luggage registered. We found out later this was a fairly pointless exercise as it remained on the tarmac in Paris when our plane departed for Sydney.

Descending through the white fluffy clouds, a mirage of colours and exotic visions assaulted the senses of those lucky enough to have window seats. A patchwork of colours and shapes defined the landscape: the iridescent blue ocean, the endless urban sprawl of Monopoly houses with their red roofs cut into the drought-stricken vegetation along with the grey arteries of interminable roads, clogged to a standstill with too many cars. As the plane made its final descent, circling and swooping down to the runway, the distinctive shapes of the white sails of the Sydney Opera House and the Coathanger — the Sydney

Harbour Bridge — were clearly visible and my heart skipped a beat. There was a general intake of breath from everyone in the plane.

Exhausted, cranky and cold, we exited from the customs area of Sydney International Airport with no luggage and no warm clothing. For the next twenty-four hours we wore an assemblage of clothing found in my father's drawers and cupboards, a new uniform of flannelette pyjamas, a cashmere sweater and an assortment of woolly socks. By the time the luggage turned up we were more than ready to attack Sydney: the shops, the restaurants, the ferries, the beaches in winter — and this of course was before we met all the family and friends who were queued up to see Mimi and Harry and their French friend.

Raphaël's eyes were permanently on swivel sticks. It was cultural overload. Living in a small village in the heartland of Provence, it was difficult for him to begin to comprehend life in a large metropolis like Paris, a place that was well known to him through movies, documentaries and the news. Sydney was an alien planet: a completely different way of life, food, language and culture.

When Harry was little the first word that he read aloud unassisted had been with me while shopping in the supermarket: 'Tim Tam' he cried for joy, throwing several packets into the trolley. So it was no surprise when Raphaël uttered the same word with sheer delight, rubbing his stomach and giving me the universal thumbs-up sign of approval, when eating a Tim Tam for the first time. Ah yes, Australian cuisine is so good, he sighed over and over. Vast quantities of taste sensations were offered to the trio of bottomless pits; the stars were lamingtons and pavlovas. Sugar and chocolate — an international language to any young person. Asian food was becoming our staple diet and I wondered how I would be able to reproduce anything like it back in Provence, where we ate mainly tomatoes, zucchini and eggplants.

We began the treadmill of visiting family and friends: Sue and Rob from Clontarf, followed by Sue and Rob from Davidson. The children were keen to see Raymond even though I wanted him dead, injured or maimed. It was arranged that we would meet at Manly. After a curt nod and a desultory wave of the hand, Raymond took the trio off on a speedboat ride around Sydney Harbour, a walk around the Opera House, lunch at McDonald's followed by yet another walk but this time across the Harbour Bridge to Luna Park, an amusement park where they spent the best part of five hours on the rides. The call I had in the early evening was not the one I wanted. They were seated at a restaurant, just minutes from Jack's house. I was to bring clean clothes for one of the boys who had been violently ill. Of course I was invited to stay for dinner — if I really wanted.

The contract for the book had been signed, which after all had been the object of our journey. By the end of our excursion in Sydney Raphaël had fallen in love with Sydney and I knew for the first time in decades that I was no longer in love with Raymond. It is difficult for love to flourish if there is no respect, and both had disappeared off the horizon. The same feeling applied when I went to pay a scheduled visit to the family home. My love for the house had died. It was evident that housekeeping was not high on the tenants' priorities, as the agent said with a wry smile — even he was shocked at the state of the house. Under no circumstances could this property be sold with them as sitting tenants; it would scare potential buyers away.

The market was scorching, with prices shooting up month by month — but only for quality properties. Buyers were desperate for houses but they were informed and discerning in their quest; a property like mine as it stood would not interest them in the slightest. It was time to cut the ties that bound us to Sydney forever. The house had to be repaired and sold as soon as possible. It was time to go home. Back to a very hot Provençal summer.

~~

It was difficult to reacclimatise to the heat of July after the windy, cold days in the southern hemisphere. The crowds and the traffic in Sydney had astounded me. I couldn't believe that I used to love battling across the sprawling city of Sydney, driving in circles to find a car space for shopping and spending hours in queues at the supermarket. I was ecstatic to be back in Apt, my sleepy French country town with its 13,000 inhabitants. During July and August, though, it is quite believable that the population must double if not sometimes triple with the foreign invasion, everyone shopping at the same time in the same supermarket. The roads were clogged with cars, trucks and bikes all heading in different directions; tempers were frayed as the mercury climbed higher and higher. It was easier to make early morning visits to the supermarket while the tourists were still in their beds and spend the rest of the time waiting out the summer, taking long afternoon naps that stretched into the evening and washing and ironing in the cool of the night. Summertime meant ferrying the children around to visit friends or paying visits to the public pool in the village.

But this summer, for the first time no one was invited to the house for lunches or dinners. The atmosphere was like a morgue. I tried not to think about Raymond, but turning the page, ruling a line under a huge chapter in my life, was exceedingly hard. The reality was that I did not want to accept change. Few people knew of my success with a publishing house accepting the manuscript because few knew that I spent my days writing. I had gone out of my way to disassociate myself from the English-speaking community, but now I was beginning to think that I had made a huge mistake.

Lizzie had taken her children for an extended trip to Australia. Deirdre had also gone to Australia to visit her family and to initiate the necessary steps for a rapid return to Queensland; personal belongings and books were packed, furniture was sold, and the rest would go into a garage sale. Kit was busy with work, and although he had managed to cut back on his punishing schedule, he was never available for dinner. Everyone else seemed to be taking refuge from the crippling heat by fleeing back to England for quick visits.

During summer, Harry continued with a couple of hours of tuition from Anne George each week to bring him up to the required standard for his first year in high school. Maybe because I had nothing to do with the activity, or maybe due to a growth spurt, Harry suddenly progressed in leaps and bounds. I could see that if I could convince Anne George, she should remain part of Harry's educational program for the next couple of years — if not until he was at least twenty-five. Declensions of verbs and exercises in French grammar had very limited appeal, whereas swimming at the local pool did, so her ability to keep Harry at his task was admirable. As with everything that Harry attacked, he took on the fundamentals of the French language with grace and charm, never complaining about the futility of the exercise.

The greatest difference between Australia and Provence is the delineation of the seasons. In general, Australian weather shifts rapidly between extremes: very hot, very wet, very dry or very windy. In Provence the weather changes every twelve weeks almost to the day. Spring and autumn were delightful, summer was unbearably hot and winter bitterly cold. Mother Nature was always on the move. With school starting back in the first week of September, autumn was already in preparation — it is one of the most vibrant times in the Luberon, with the rich colours and the light on the distant hills, the soft luminosity and warmth of the twilight. The fields lay fallow, ready for the first of the autumn rains, and the tractors stood in readiness to tear the earth up in large clods in preparation for the next crop. Green vine leaves were in abundance, the large purple grapes ripening on the vines before the harvest. With the sound of the municipal pool being emptied and the grating of the chairs being stacked in tidy piles to go into winter hibernation, everyone breathed easier as the summer drew to a close.

The holidays were finally coming to an end. I was sent to the high school with a list of things that needed my cheques or signature. Hours were spent in the queue at the local photography shop having passport photos taken so that they could be attached to every piece of identification that was deemed necessary by the school and other establishments. My bag was spewing forth an unstoppable river of documents for the children. Electricity accounts to prove that I existed and lived where I said I lived, photocopies of marriage, birth and death certificates, vaccination certificates, medical certificates to ensure that there was no reason why they should not attend sport or swimming classes. The list was endless, but finally the first day of high school began for Harry. It was also his birthday, and in his unconquerable way, instead of being upset by this fact he was positively joyous, because he would be seeing all of his friends.

It began as usual with the parents standing around in the playground. As Monsieur Gallegos, the principal of the school, called out each child's name, they lined up behind their new teacher, who then took them off into the maze of corridors and stairs to the sound of loud applause from the parents. Our babies had started high school. Many mothers had to look the other way, dabbing their eyes as their darlings sauntered past them, smirking, to their awaiting future.

Our days were now revolving around homework, travelling to Anne's house ten kilometres away in Rustrel, and rewriting large sections of my manuscript that needed reworking. I had gone back to the routine of waking early so that my writing could be done in peace and quiet. Alcohol was banned until all work on the manuscript was completed. Writing about your own life is a peculiar activity, as it forces you to look at things objectively and with the knowledge of hindsight. If I wanted to be honest with myself, the relationship with Raymond was dead in the water after he left us in France in 2001. He had come to live with us as a favour to an old friend and lover, nothing more. I had not read the signs. Or rather, I could have read the signs but I was determined to ignore them. There was already so much change in our lives. An enormous amount of good fortune had followed us since we had come to Provence for the first time in January 2000. Now I could see that I had been on an egocentric belly-button gazing trip, caught up in my world of me. Somehow I had lost sight of the fact that every house in the valley contained a family struggling with its own dramas, triumphs and failures.

~

A call came from the Sydney real estate office to ask me what was to be done with our personal items that remained in the family home before it went on the market. Rather than wisely saying 'donate everything to charity', I was overcome with a desire to see the house for one last time before it was sold. I would travel to Sydney yet again, a five-day trip just before Christmas.

Claire understood my need to say goodbye to a house that meant so much to me although, as family homes go, the children and I had lived in it for a very short time. It represented my first step of independence; the first decision that I had made as a widow with two little children. The location had been decided because of my happy childhood memories and the proximity to the private schools of which my husband would have thoroughly approved. Now it represented the only way that I could dig myself out of my temporary financial quagmire. Claire said that she would give me a compass for Christmas, so that I would find my way home and find my way in life. We both laughed at this, but deep down, it struck a chord. I had no idea what I was doing running back to Sydney. Everyone held their breath, hoping that Raymond would not be involved yet again.

The moment I walked through my father's house crying out that I was home, I realised that I had made a monumental mistake. The colours were all wrong. I was in the wrong time zone. I was waking up in French time. I certainly was not home. The forthcoming sale of my house was completely under control and organised, right down to the colour and type of flowers ordered for the massive vases. There was one small, final thing to deal with: the storage boxes under the house had to be sorted and the contents given away or thrown into the bin. After callously stripping away our worldly goods over the years, there were scant possessions left to deal with. Sorting through photographs of the children, rocking horses and Mimi's doll house would not take up a lot of time, but it would take an enormous amount of emotional energy. I couldn't move some of the larger items by myself, so the only male who I said would never be needed again in my life came to my rescue. Raymond and I unearthed photos of Mimi and Harry, the children that he considered to be almost his own, not in name or in blood, but in love. Images of the children in various costumes and poses and at different ages lay scattered on the floorboards around us; we sat on the polished wooden steps with our arms around each other, unable to say anything. Saying goodbye was now long overdue. Trying to kiss the tears that were streaming down my face, Raymond asked if I would join him the following month in Rome for a study trip.

'Raymond, don't you get it? In opera, you know it is the end when the fat lady comes out and sings. Well, she has been singing for years. It is just that we have never heard her.'

CHAPTER NINETEEN

The Farewell Tour

Once the family house had been visited and the remaining personal items distributed across Sydney to friends and family, there was very little left to do. Dropping off the sewing machine to my friend Liz in Whale Beach, I could not help but take a drive around the area where Norman and I had spent so many happy times before he became tragically ill. There were places where we had been together in the 1980s before our marriage and then in the 1990s when the children were born. Everything looked exactly the same. The sparkling Pacific Ocean was enticing, the long sandy beaches ready for the summer Christmas invasion. I needed to see the house where we lived in the leafy suburb of Bilgola, high above Bilgola Beach in a small road with very little traffic. While I sat parked outside the house a man approached me: 'Are you lost? Which street are you looking for, love?'

'No. Everything is fine. Not lost at all. I know

exactly where I live and now I know exactly what I am doing. I am going home to France to be with my children. Merry Christmas.'

I took one last look at our old home and said goodbye. It was full of happy memories, but as my mother used to say, home is always in your heart. You carry it wherever you go. I was ready to head back to France. Everyone was so busy with Christmas preparations that it was clear that my presence, although welcomed, was not particularly wanted. I kissed Kate and her family goodbye and brought forward my departure date, leaving without any hesitation.

Claire and the children had given me an ultimatum: I had to be back for Christmas. Once again I was exhausted from the massive dose of plane travel but nevertheless I was home. I stood in the howling wind on the Avignon station platform waiting for Claire, two days before Christmas, jet-lagged and drained. The cold had seeped into my bones; not even a hot bath, even if we had a bath at our home, would help. I had left Sydney sweltering under hot summer skies, but the romantic yearnings I had had for wintry scenery with Christmas lights sparkling as the snowflakes fell had been eradicated by a ten-minute wait without an adequate coat in the freezing cold.

Mimi and Harry had been on the telephone to me before I had left Sydney, in raptures over this year's Christmas light extravaganza, which was even more

spectacular than the previous year's. Silhouettes, fairy
lights and garlands festooned the main street, hanging
precariously from the huge plane trees and monuments
in Apt. *Joyeuses Fêtes* and other season greetings were
written up in neon lights and strung across the streets,
and cascading curtains of minuscule white lights
bedecked the town hall; everything glittered and
dazzled, flashed and throbbed. Christmas was in full
force. Everyone looked skywards for the first signs of
snow, but though the temperature continued to
plummet below zero, the skies remained icy blue and
bereft of anything that resembled a snow cloud.

I had discovered, to my horror, that the man with
the thick accent whose name I had thought was Jungpo
was not an electrician but the head of a large
corporation which provided the lights that decorated
the Eiffel Tower and just about every monument in
France — and many other major international cities,
for that matter. As a goodwill gesture, he decorated Apt
with the latest and the best decorations every year. This
year the company had outdone itself. Since our first
meeting at Pierre and Kamila's in Saignon, our paths
had crossed occasionally; every time he was incredibly
charming, but his accent was almost incomprehensible.
Ever since I started to learn languages as a young
woman, my Achilles heel has always been my difficulty
understanding men in French or Italian — men have a
tendency to mumble, articulating poorly. It was bad

enough face to face but on the telephone it was sometimes impossible. Jean-Paul, or Jungpo as I thought of him, fell solidly into this category. Most of our conversations had been mere snippets concerning weather or health — both subjects that I could easily handle. Luckily, our social interaction did not extend to long conversations that ranged across sex, politics or religion.

I mulled over New Year's resolutions for 2005 that were vaguely acceptable and achievable while trying to organise the Christmas festivities — which were on the way to being even worse than the previous year according to the children, who would not allow me to wallow in a jet-lag stupor. In less than forty-eight hours, I was expected to shop, decorate the house, invite the guests, put up the tree, cook the turkey, and shuck the oysters. For their part, they were prepared to check that the fire did not die out while they watched hours of television with their arms around the necks of Zorro and Rosie — after all, they were on holidays.

During this period I had long talks on the phone with my sister Kate, someone who understood what true love was all about. She had married her teenage sweetheart and true love was alive and flourishing in her home almost three decades later. 'You just don't get it, do you? Of course Raymond loves you. He adores you. He will always be there for you and the kids but he just doesn't love you enough. You have to be able to

compromise and give up some of the dreams. That's
how you make the glue that sticks you together. And by
the way, you are just as bad as he is. You never wanted to
live together in Sydney and now you are in France. If
you wanted things to work you wouldn't have stayed
there. Hen, true love might be a place rather than a
person for you. Have you ever thought that just maybe
you are more in love with France than with Raymond?'

And so there it was. There was my resolution for
2005. Page turning, line ruling or whatever my sister
wanted to call it. Move on to a new phase in my life.
The children watched me like hawks to see if I was
coping and were extremely surprised when I
announced that Raymond would be coming to visit in
mid-February after his course had finished in Rome.

It was a testing time. He was desperate to see the
children. He too, had some farewells to make: a long
goodbye to the Luberon, our animals and the café
where he had spent far too many afternoons with Kit.
Of course the hardest thing would be to say goodbye to
the children. Mimi and Harry observed that for the first
time, there was a certain amount of coolness or
aloofness between us, which was from sheer self-
preservation, as we tried to tell them that this would be
our last holiday together as a family unit. My heart and
soul had shut down completely to Raymond. On the
Saturday morning of his departure, the four of us were
in the café with Deidre having a final drink before a

wander around the market and maybe a farewell lunch with Kit and Deirdre. Raymond stood in front of me holding out a massive bouquet of flowers that he and Harry had just bought from my favourite florist.

'So Raymond, are you coming back for summer this year?' Deirdre is very straight-shooting.

Raymond looked balefully at me, holding out the flowers.

'No, Deirdre. This is Raymond's last trip to visit us here. He will never come back.' I needed to jump in and answer for Raymond in case he said something that I would regret.

'Ha, never say never.' Deirdre sniffed loudly as she watched Raymond hold out the bouquet towards me.

'Happy Valentine's Day, my darling.' The children hang from his neck as he held out the bunch of yellow flowers. The children silently mimicked the words 'my darling', kissing the air passionately while running their arms up and down their own backs.

'Since when has he called her "my darling"?' Mimi whispered none too softly to her brother through the layers of her thick woollen scarf.

The image of the happy family was so strong, yet the emotions no longer fitted the picture. I prayed that the predicted snow would not arrive and impede Raymond's departure time. Freedom was calling us both. Finally, I no longer needed to have a man in my life to determine my future or my happiness. Provence had given me the freedom to discover who I was and the things that were needed to make me stable and content: it was not a man — a husband or a lover. As the train pulled out of the station, for the first time, I was honestly delighted to see Raymond leave. There were no tears or sadness. A new future filled with freedom and independence was calling. Five days later, I saw Harry throwing the bouquet of yellow roses into the garbage bag. '*Maman*, I thought that it was time to chuck these out. It was thoughtful of Raymond but you would think that he would know after all these years that you hate yellow roses and yellow daisies. I guess that it is better to have nothing than something you really don't like.'

~~

Winter was bitterly cold. The landscape was barren and bleak but that was not at all how I felt. Life was good: my inner sea was calm. I was a single mother with no immediate support lines, but after ten years of widowhood, I had learnt to stand completely on my own. Independent. I made a plan to keep myself occupied for the next six months, and under no circumstances would I indicate to anyone that I was available for love and romance. I waited for spring and the warmth that accompanies the blossoms on the cherry trees, the intense colours and sounds of bees in the blossoms. I knew that with spring things change and hearts are restored and mended.

Winter meant spending some time with friends in Saignon. In a moment of weakness one morning over a cup of steaming black coffee and a buttery croissant from Christine's bakery in Saignon, I mentioned to Kamila that I was feeling positive and optimistic but at the same time it was extremely difficult to get by without the constant stream of emails or calls from Raymond. I missed having someone there. My idea of standing alone had been extremely good in theory but it was proving to be quite demanding in practice. As usual, she clicked her tongue, telling me that spring was on its way: a time for love. No matter the time of day, Kamila is always ready to give some sort of firm philosophical argument for any situation; so convincing are her arguments that you are easily swayed to her way of thinking. Early March, however, in my view, was still too early for spring and for love.

Later that evening the telephone rang and a male's voice in extremely odd English asked for me: 'Hello, *madame*. I am presenting myself to you. You are knowing me. You are knowing me from the house of Pierre and Kamila. Kamila, she is telling me that you are so sad and lonely. I would like the occasion to make a little dinner with you and give you a good time.'

It is very difficult to keep a straight face and not laugh outright when English is abused in such a manner. I kept thinking how my French must have sounded in the early days when I was learning the rudiments of the language — and probably still does, as I continue to make ridiculous mistakes. This man hadn't even told me his name yet. I had no intention of letting some stranger take me to dinner for a 'good time'. I would kill Kamila next time I saw her. Vicious thoughts of murdering my Polish friend filled my head. But in broken English, the mystery man continued determinedly: 'You are not liking a finger in your ring, non? Non, *je veux dire* no, what I mean is a ring on your finger. Or maybe my hat I throw on your ring?' This was becoming more and more bizarre. I could not contain my mirth.

'Stop. Just a minute. I think, well I hope, that you mean that you are not interested in marrying me but you are throwing your hat in the ring.' It was starting to click who this was. Bloody hell, it was Jungpo! I got out my finger and itemised my response.

'Look, *monsieur*, thank you for your call — and I must ring Kamila to thank her as well. Let me make this as clear as possible:

1. *I do not want to join your harem of adoring females.*
2. *I am not interested in being your mistress.*
3. *I do not want your fingers anywhere near me.*
4. *No one is throwing their hat in the ring to be counted as a prospective lover because —*

5. *I do not sleep with Frenchmen. In fact, I do not want to sleep with anyone, or as you French say, take some afternoon delight. I say 'no' to learning the Provençal Pirouette with you. I am very flattered but* non, merci — *no thank you.*

6. *Talking about thank you, I have to end our conversation on a positive note and say that you are so wonderfully generous with the Christmas lights. I know that they bring so much pleasure to so many people.*

I thought that was clear and concise. I had politely but firmly put him back in his box. There was no way I would have anything to do with this man — especially if he continued to speak in English.

'*Madame*, yes, the lists, she are very good to clear the mind, *n'est-ce pas?* You are impressing with my English. I have been going many times to *Ecosse*, how you say it, ah *oui* Scotland, I have been learning it there very quickly. Tomorrow I am free for lunch. You come to the big gates. House with olive trees. Yes, *madame*, I am living in house opposite road to you. I am being your neighbour.'

And so began one of the most wonderful friendships. Over the following weeks, I discovered that I could decipher Jungpo's French better than his English and that we had many interests in common. He was an avid reader, connoisseur of fine wine and had a beautiful house, fabulous pool and central heating. I, on the other hand, loved to write, drink and swim in other people's pools and had inadequate heating in my home. Jungpo had never studied Latin and had no interest in the symbols of Polyphemus in the nymphaeum of Claudius, which made a refreshing change. Now all I had to do was retrain my brain to call him his correct name.

CHAPTER TWENTY

Stripped Bare

The heat was rising up from the asphalt, shimmering and dancing in transparent chimeras. Such midday heat was not typical for a late spring day, even in the south of France. My book, bottle of sunscreen and the small black automatic gate-opener rattled together in the depths of my gaily striped tote bag, slightly muffled by the large towel that took up most of the space.

Foolishly, I had decided to walk rather than drive the short distance, in an effort to keep some sort of physical exercise in my daily regimen. Instead of a vigorous walk it had turned into a slow amble as I hopped and jumped over the large puddles of rainwater from the unpredicted downpour the previous evening. It was the beginning of our fifth year living here in France and my fourth year running my small business, and it had become increasingly rare to have the time to enjoy a few of the sensual pleasures that are offered in so many forms in

Provence; a walk in the French countryside was definitely one of them.

The snow-white flowers from the cherry trees had fallen, blown off by the fierce Mistral, and were now replaced by the small round buds that would miraculously turn into luminous fat red cherries within a few weeks, bringing van loads of itinerant gypsies for the harvest. As well as the bees that buzzed continuously, some would say that love was in the air: happiness certainly was. The wonderful warm sunny days that heralded the end of winter had been late this year, but as the temperature continued to rise, spring had sprung.

Going over to the intercom that was discreetly placed at one side of the high dry stone Provençal wall, I took a deep breath and reached out to press the switch. Silence. Far in the distance, through the bars of the gates, I could make out one if not two figures in deep discussion. One was prodding the large clods of friable earth with a large stick, and the other figure, obscured almost completely by the corner of the chicken coop, appeared to be listening intently. The subject of their conversation seemed to be the stripling olive trees and when to begin the planting. The spring rain had been provident, unexpected and torrential; a strong earthy smell still lingered in the rising midday heat. A small prick of irritation pierced my general feeling of tranquillity and happiness; there was no doubt, I was beginning to have difficulties with my eyesight. One of the figures was lean and tall; no doubt it was the gardener, André, but the other figure could easily have been man or beast, most likely his dog. Vanity would never allow me to wear glasses. I preferred to mistake distant dogs for people.

My instructions were that if no one replied I was to make myself at home beside the pool. The owner of the house, my neighbour, would join me if time permitted, for a late lunch. My orders had been to simply enjoy myself. Food and drink would be in the fridge. Telephone and Internet connection were beside the sturdy table which had been set up for me, if I wished to work on my computer. But the real attraction was the swimming pool. I was desperate to swim. At our home we had no pool and no bath, which didn't matter, as there was no hot water in the bathroom. Luxury extended to having hot water in the shower. At a family meeting, the children and I had decided that a pool was the last thing on our list of priorities. I told the children that they should cultivate winter and summer friends, determined by who had central heating and a swimming pool. I followed the same rule, so now I was paying a neighbourly visit.

I pointed the small black cube at the command switch on the top of the gate. The large metal gates swung silently open. At the end of the path next to the house, I could see a large space devoid of any cars.

Obviously, my neighbour had been caught up at the
office and was not yet home. Across the meticulously
manicured lawn, over near the fields in the far distance
I could see André's distinctive blue and yellow car. I
crunched up the path, admiring the attention to detail
in the garden, the colours and shapes so faultless that
everything melded into perfect accord. The fishpond, I
noted with satisfaction, was infinitely smaller and less
spectacular than mine, even with its life-sized bronze
statue of a heron feeding in the reeds around the water's
edge. The simplicity and harmony of the garden was so
incredibly beautiful, it sent my senses spinning.

The pool, close to the front gates, was surrounded
by dense foliage that made it an ideal haven for any
swimmer. Although the air temperature was rising
steadily, I thought the water would still have that post-
winter chill, but I was wrong. The heating had been
activated and was taking the temperature from arctic to
tropical. Two heavy teak sun lounges with creamy-
coloured cushions had been placed closely side by side,
a beautiful cream and white linen tablecloth covered
the table set for two, a bottle of red wine older than my
daughter was placed to one side of the table. It was pure
paradise. Was it a French seduction scene or over-
generous friendship? What did it matter? For the time
being, I was alone.

I threw the contents of my tote bag across the bench
in the poolside kitchen but there was no sign of any

swimming costume. I would only find out later that I
had left it in an unceremonious heap on my bed. I had
been so excited to find it, extricating it from winter
hibernation for its first outing of the season, that I had
forgotten to pack it into the bag. Knowing that I would
be able to hear any car passing through the large metal
gates, I reasoned that I would have ample time to cover
up modestly before anyone came within close vicinity
of the pool area. I folded my chocolate silk skirt and
top in a neat pile along with my latest acquisition in
lacy lingerie. There is nothing more liberating than
swimming in the nude in the middle of a green oasis.
Nobody around. No children asking about food,
television or *Maman*'s taxi service to friends in
neighbouring villages. No thoughts or cares to cloud
my mind, just the wonderfully warm water that was
finally thawing out the cold which had seeped into my
bones during winter.

His work achieved in the organic vegetable patch
next to the olive grove, André walked across to speak to
his boss, who was sitting in the sunshine out on the
veranda in front of the kitchen. With the telephone
cradled in the crook of his neck, Jean-Paul beckoned
André to sit at the table while he went to make another
shot of strong black coffee.

'*Merci*, Claude, I will have the car collected early this
afternoon.' He finished his conversation with the garage
that had been servicing his sleek silver bullet. André was

clearly agitated. 'Jean-Paul, there is a problem. It appears that someone, well a woman, *monsieur*, there is a naked woman in your pool.' Jean-Paul insisted that everyone addressed him by his first name and used the very friendly *'tu'* form. André held his hands across his own chest imitating female bumps and lumps.

'How could that happen? How could she have broken into the property? She must have climbed over the wall. It is just not possible. I don't understand how this could happen. She is not a gypsy because she is so very white. I think that she must be German, *Monsieur* Jean-Paul. Those Germans never swim in a swimming costume. They are always stomping and cycling all over our countryside in little shorts and swim naked whenever they can. *Monsieur*, shall I call the police?'

'André, stay calm. I will deal with this matter. The police are not needed. I think that I shall deal with this myself.' A smile broke across his face.

'André, I think that you should go and check the progress of our cherries in the far field. No, wait, go with Pierre into Avignon and pick up my car from the garage. The car will be ready in the early afternoon. You are not needed this afternoon. *Merci* André.'

There was no question about it. Just as Kamila had predicted early that morning while pointing her Polish nose into the wind, with the advent of spring, something was certainly in the air.

Epilogue

My fortieth birthday was held on an unseasonable balmy June evening, only seven years late. The interior and exterior of the house was decked out with enough party lights to make the Eiffel Tower jealous. In the living room in centre place was an enormous bouquet of forty-seven red long-stemmed roses. In the late afternoon, the florist had arrived at the front gates tooting the horn. Leaping from her van, the delivery lady, sighing heavily, held out the magnificent bouquet to me. Claire and I stood in the road with our mouths hanging wide open. I had never received flowers like these in my life.

'I did this bouquet myself. He said that it had to be perfect.'

'They are beautiful.' For the first time Claire was lost for words. Her mind was ticking out loud as she tried to work out who had sent the flowers.

Without wasting a moment, the misty-eyed delivery lady read the anonymous card out loud: '"A kiss is attached to each one." It is not signed but I know who made the order. He is your neighbour.'

The caterers had arrived with a refrigerated truck, bearing enough food for weeks of nonstop eating; the champagne flowed and the noise of excited revellers was on the increase. Jungpo arrived to check that the Christmas lights had been correctly installed. He was carrying a large orange parcel tied up with chocolate brown Hermès ribbon. New friends who had been made in the past five years of our life here in France were assembled around the long tables, and the cascading fairy lights twinkled above us. Mimi and Harry were busy quaffing lemonade in champagne flutes and sticking their fingers into the dips when no one was looking. Claire was in command, reorganising the tables and doing yet another magnificent table decoration. Patrick was in charge of whipping off the champagne corks and checking that the barmen were filling up all the glasses. At the table, Jungpo sat beside me, and for the first time I understood everything that he said to me. Darkness fell and the lights twinkled through the trees. It would be a long night.

~~

Our lives continue to be intertwined with good times, excellent wine and food and fantastic friends. Vague opinions are bandied about as to when we will eventually rebuild the house, install heating, windows that shut firmly and shutters that stay on their hinges, and hire the plumber to fix the leaky bath, the toilet and the hot water in the hand basin.

The properties are now up and running, with a devoted clientele who return year after year, making the financial aspect more solid but the constant grind of keeping everything in working order and maintained keeps me on my toes.

Claire's daughters are finding their way in life and her son Raphaël continues to have brilliant academic results, moving with ease into his next phase as a young man. Mimi and Harry continue to be a delight and the sole reason for my existence. They look for fun wherever they can find it and tease me mercilessly.

Provence has been the exotic backdrop to all of my life over the past five years. The beauty, the colours, the change of seasons sweep into your psyche without you being aware until one day the very thought of leaving this land fills you with dread, and you know that it is time to start thinking seriously about digging your feet deep into the Provençal soil.

If you have enjoyed *Lavender and Linen*, you will also like Henrietta Taylor's first book.

ESCAPING

As a young woman, Australian-born Henrietta Taylor searched the world for Mr Right: the perfect husband with whom she could have a happy family and a house with a white picket fence. When she met the affable Norman, her dreams all seemed to come true. But then disaster struck, leaving her a bereft widow with two small children and little idea of how to look after them — or herself.

Searching for a different life, she packed her bags and took the children off to France, where she had found romance and adventure many years before. But what seemed so simple once is now complicated by feelings of loss, and the reappearance of the man she calls the Latin Lover.

In a tiny village in the south of France, Veuve (Widow) Taylor, as she is known, finds a new circle of friends, an unexpected role as the proprietor of three charming guesthouses, and a different version of family life. Along the way she discovers that the path to happiness can sometimes turn into a very unconventional journey.

Told with candour and refreshingly self-deprecating humour, *Escaping* is the story of a fairytale gone wrong — its tragic consequences, and its surprising and triumphant aftermath.